What is Thinking?
And Other Philosophical Reflections

Saitya Brata Das

What is Thinking?: And Other Philosophical Reflections
Saitya Brata Das

First Published 2021

ISBN 978-93-5002-686-1

Published by
AAKAR BOOKS
28 E Pocket IV, Mayur Vihar Phase I
Delhi 110 091 India
aakarbooks@gmail.com

Laser Typeset at
Sakshi Computers, Delhi

Printed at
Sapra Brothers, Noida

For

My Mother

Contents

Acknowledgements

With the exception of the first essay "What is thinking?" the other essays included in this book were published previously, most of these essays being the earliest works that I have ever written and are no longer in circulation (apart from the first, second and the third). This is the reason for bringing them up once again to the public visibility so that insights gained therein are not lost in the pages of the bygone issues of scholarly journals. Therefore, instead of trying to make them up-to-date—for I have meanwhile gone beyond much of the insights gained therein—I have decided to keep them as they are, apart from correcting some grammatical mistakes and typographical errors. I acknowledge the following publishers for allowing me to republish these essays:

1. "…And this palpitation of existence" in *South Asian Ensemble* (2015), Vol. 7, No. 1&2, pp. 133-140.
2. "When religion has (not) returned?" in *Margins—A Journal of Literature and Culture*, VII-VIII (Gauhati University Press, 2017-18), pp. 25-40.
3. "(Dis)Figures of death: taking the side of Derrida, taking the side of death" in *Derrida Today* (Edinburgh: Edinburgh University Press, May 2010), Vol. 3: 1, pp. 1-20.

4. "The abyss of human freedom" in *Journal for Indian Council of Philosophical Research* (October 2010), Vol. XXVII, No. 4, pp. 91-104.
5. "Derrida's tympan: mourning, philosophy, literature" in *Research and Criticism*, Banaras Hindu University Journal (Pencraft 2010), Vol. 1, pp. 23-34.
6. "Wholly otherwise" in *Journal for Cultural Research* (London: Routledge, Taylor and Francis), 12: 2, (2008: 167-180).
7. "Of force, of rhythm, of melody" in *Language Forum* (Delhi: Bahri, 2004), Vol. 30, No. 2, 11-25.

What is thinking?

Dialectic comes to a standstill

What does it mean to ask what thinking is?: this seems to be the ineluctable question that poses itself to us even before we ask ourselves 'what is thinking'? What is the nature of this thinking which is concerned, above all, with what thinking itself is? Is not it too obvious a "thing", so we wonder, that we call "thinking" which we all "do" anyway spontaneously, early in the morning and late at night? And we always think and every day, without having to be concerned with what thinking itself is? Is it not too self-evident and immediately recognizable a phenomenon, and hence unproblematic a thing—that we think, and that this "thing" called "thinking" we do all the time, as spontaneously as eating and drinking and sleeping? Is it worthy enough of a problem or a question for us to be concerned with when there are much more serious, urgent and important, much more relevant and unavoidable problems that beset us today and daily make us thoughtful to the point of anguish and despair? Is not it rather symptomatic of the bourgeois inertia of arm-chair intellectuals who spend the whole day, every day, from morning till evening, in closed office rooms, thinking about "thinking"? 'Thinking does not change the world; the task is to change the world': so we are so told, from right to the left side, from the left to the right. It appears that thinking is only an impotent cry of a beautiful soul, the unending sigh of an "unhappy consciousness", the intellectual luxury of a privileged few who can afford to think about thinking. Thus, it is deduced it is the most irrelevant task of thinking today to think of what thinking itself, *as such,* may at all be like.

Moreover, we do not at all have time. It appears that the world needs immediate mending, and our immediate action alone can do that. We need to gather forces and mobilize individuals into programmable political actions to achieve a definite goal: a voice to be heard in the parliament; a policy is to be passed in the executive councils; a certain negotiations to be achieved, etc. The world appears to be running out of time, and we daily live out our life without respite. If the world today is to be understood in a phrase, nothing appears to be better than that it is governed by "the metaphysics of speed". Our time is constantly running out, in a sense that is entirely opposed to that of St. Paul's messianic urgency. St. Paul was eagerly waiting for the imminent second coming of Christ and for the eschatological judgment of all; today's godless world, on the other hand, does not need to stand (at least it believes so) up to the divine judgment: since the death of God, the world has now become "secular" and fearless; as aboriginal and autochthonous, this pantheistic world does not need any legitimation of its being apart from its own immanence. Fearlessly the human Subject of this earth now rules over the whole earthly existence like the sovereign monarch.

Moreover, we do not at all have time. Today in news channel debates, in academic debates and executive councils of Universities, in our parliaments about crucial decisions, even if it's about abolition of a state, we do not have time to think and critically engage with issues. Rather we must decide *hic et nunc*, with an unequivocal "yes" or "no", without taking up time, without debates and discussions. "Do you think the state is to be abolished?: say 'yes' or 'no'?" Decision is about one word, and that must be an unequivocal either/or: either 'yes' or 'no'.

In other words, we are at the time of exception: it is time itself that is constantly running out, and this running out of time is the constant and normative exception in today's exceptional world. Our sovereign figure in councils must decide immediately about the fate of the world, for the world is running out of time, and there is no respite. It appears as if we are at the end of the world, at the apocalyptic extremity of time, at the edge of the earth, and we do not have time to pause a little, and ask ourselves: what does it mean to think? To spend time on this question appears like most useless expenditure of time: to students, it does not offer any grade; to the professor, it does not give any profit to his ever climbing on the ladder of success. And yet, it is precisely the task of the professor or the student to be concerned with this ancient, and yet ever new question precisely because of the irresolvable enigma that it poses, and precisely because it is concerned with the very fundamental problematic of human existence.

Through this censoring of our taking up of time in our "unnecessary" philosophical discussions and thinking—a censoring that is supposedly made by well-intentioned authorities who give themselves the "messianic" task to mend the world (which, according to them, does not need unnecessary thinking), through this very of censoring of thinking, something about thinking suddenly show themselves to us: *to think is to have time.* 'Thinking makes us solitary and slow', as the solitary and slow thinker Martin Heidegger remarks. In a world running out of time, thinking (that is concerned with thinking itself) thus manifests itself as something anachronistic and disturbing: the moment thinking takes another time apart from the time of the world, and the moment thinking makes another movement apart from the programmable, economic movement of the world-running-out-of-time—thinking suddenly becomes a disturbing presence. For the world likes to be all that there is: total, complete in itself, without outside, and constantly having to run out. Then, suddenly comes a thinking which is not the one we are usually familiar with (ratiocinative thinking concerned with the programmable action in sight to achieve a definite political-economic goal), and a space opens up that is, in a way, outside the "world", a space of the outside that refuses to coincide with our world as it exists (a space outside the world in which we live out our habitual mode of being, the world which is commensurable with our life as we habitually live out). In relation to the world running out of time, this new thinking (which is also more ancient than all the recent thoughts that are making in news today) is incredibly slow and solitary: *an-chronos*, as if without time, anachronistic. The solitude of time thus appears to be something essential about this new—but also ancient—thinking: a momentary halt of time, a confrontation with something in the "sudden" of its appearance (as Plato speaks in his *Parmenides*), an eruption of the moment that, in its appearance, comes as it were to arrest time and to make it standstill. Such a sudden moment sets us apart from ourselves, and makes us *the apart* self: it is the partitioning of time, a separation of time; it is *the moment* which separates itself from the homogenous time of the world. Somehow who experiences this *sudden* becomes the solitary one who thinks what thinking itself is.

May be we are doing rather too much? Maybe there is too much action happening around us which is unceasingly, moment by moment, changing the modern world wherein we live, the world which is constantly living off at its end, at the constant point of its imminent disappearance? Maybe we are doing too much and not thinking enough? May be what appears to be self-evident and all-too-relevant is not evident enough? May be we need to be blind at times, like Oedipus, to see the truth (to be like "Oedipus who has eyes too many", as the poet Hölderlin poetizes)? Being at the end of the modern world, or, rather being "thrown" at this end, maybe we have not yet begun to think the essential? Being tyrannized by the immediate urgency of too much action, and being tyrannized by the blinding light of self-evidence, maybe have not started to think yet (thinking that makes us not only solitary and slow but renders the self-evident riddle-some, enigmatic and mysterious)? Perhaps!

Perhaps! It is this *perhaps* that does not seem to belong quite confidently to the knowledge of the world. 'Why is something rather than not?': with this Schelling asks the very fundamental question of philosophy. At once enigmatic and simple, such questions do not anymore appear to belong to the economy of the world-running-out-of-time; for it is not that these questions will take a lot of time, but that time itself does not sufficiently measure up to the demand of these questions. Only the sudden of the moment momentarily catches up with the eternal flame of a fundamental question, only to leave the question unresolved once again. To leave something unresolved: this is not the mode in which the economy of the world operates. By reducing all reflections and thinking to the ratiocinative solving of the solvable questions, the modern world has left behind all fundamental and essential questions of thinking and of life, and has given up philosophical contemplations to the violence of cognition. The metaphysics of the modern world is thus indelibly marked with this violence of cognition that seeks to seize life in all possible aspects, and totalize them in the form of a system. For there is a violence of cognition that demands, tyrannically, an immediate intelligibility of a phenomenon so as to be able to grasp it, to able to name it, to fix forever—under the force of law, by the power of the concept, under the newly made rules by the current regime that rules over us as the lord of our life and death. 'Recognize the law, or meet your death': the sovereign tells us. Do we have freedom to say "no" to this imperative? Who does not recognize, immediately, in utter lucidity, this "truth"?: such is this immediate identity made between law and death! The force of the law lies in the very work of death. In the regime of the law, life is not to be found: this is the price that the human civilization has paid, and has never ceased paying, to be able to grasp the world in knowledge at the price of thinking. All essential thinking, on the other hand, is an *indication* and a *showing* (not a grasping) towards something radically unknown and unknowable, not that it may pass over into knowledge one day but one that remains as radical non-knowledge.

Such is the movement of philosophical thinking (as *showing*) to be found in Plato's dialogues: through dialectical question-answer, Socrates leads the interlocutors to the point of the most enigmatic non-knowledge, to the point where knowledge comes to a standstill, and here the philosopher leaves off his interlocutors to perdure in the most unnamable marvel and wonder. Beginning with his distinction between two modes of ignorance—the Socratic ignorance (who knows that he does not know) and the ignorance of the Sophists (that they do not know that they do not know, while all the time presuming that they know what they know)—the dialectic moves ahead to the moment when, suddenly, all the presumption of knowledge (on the part of the Sophists) comes to a standstill, and the dialectic comes to a halt. A sudden eruption of the exuberant leaves the interlocutors speechless who, till now, were only too garrulous: the *hubris* of knowledge now suddenly appears like chatter, devoid of substance, that constantly feeds on empty thoughts. This humility, this emptying of knowledge, this *kenosis* (self-emptying) of force is the necessary moment of all essential thinking. Thus, Socrates does not lead his interlocutors to more and more knowledge; rather, Socrates/Platonic dialectic is a pedagogic strategy to empty our knowledge to open up to what is greater than cognition, that is, to the radical non-knowledge in the philosophical contemplation of eternity. In this way, the violence of cognition is repaired, and our being itself is redeemed by the philosophical contemplation of the excess, of the surplus, of the infinity outside all totality of cognition. Redemption: this is the task of all essential thinking, of philosophical thinking, of poetic contemplation of eternity.

Thus, there is a qualitative distinction to be made between the philosopher and the sophist. The philosopher is the ignorant one; only thing she knows is that she knows nothing. On the other hand, the business of the sophist is to know. Now that the philosopher does not know does not merely say about the condition of her intellectual existence (that she does not know); it is rather the very task of her entire existence—*not* to know. A strange task it is: how *not* to know, for everyone knows inevitably, including the philosopher? In a deeper sense, the philosopher's non-knowledge is—in distinction from the Sophists' knowledge—is the highest knowledge: to know that one does not know is the highest knowledge possible for a mortal being. It is something like what Nicholas de Cusa would say as "learned knowledge" (*docta ignorantia*): for the Socratic knowledge is at once a radical ignorance. The dialectical movement is not just a technical procedure of knowledge: it defines the very *amour*, the very *erotic* of the search by which Socrates, by the very appeal of his ugliness, leads his interlocutors to the contemplation of transcendent beauty. The ugly Socrates seduces the beautiful youths of Athens to the contemplation of the Beauty as such, of the Good without being. The ugliest man of Greece (an anachronism!) is also the most erotic individual of Athens: he is enraptured in wonder by the vision of beauty beyond all being. The Sophist, on the other hand, is a technician of knowledge of what is presently available in the world; he is the bureaucrat of action who is busy in the thoughtless organization of the world as it already exists. Lacking the ecstasy, the enthusiasm (*enthousiasmos*: the one who is possessed by God) and the creative madness (through which, as Socrates says, all the beautiful things have come to Greece), the all-too-rational-calculative-profit-making Sophist is analogues to the existentially bankrupt, spiritually impoverished, utterly banal and uncreative human being in our modern civilization. That we are no longer able to pose fundamental questions of human existence in any essential manner shows, more than anything else, the sheer wasteland of the modern civilization, its utter banality and spiritual bankruptcy. In the last pages of his *The Ages of the World* Schelling tells us that there are three kinds of mad individuals that exist: there is someone mad who is *really* mad, who has reached beyond the uttermost moment of sobriety, and thus can create nothing at all; then there is the all-too-rational individual who, having no touch of madness in him, can create nothing new, and is intellectually-existentially the sterile one (the technician of empty knowledge, the bureaucrat of action who constantly arranges and re-arranges the same world in perfect obedience to sovereign powers); then there is the individual who, constantly solicitated to madness, regulates that madness and creates something new, beautiful and creative. It is this last one of whom Plato speaks of when he said that all that is beautiful and creative has come out of a 'divine madness'.

'The banality of evil'

'Recognize the law, or meet your death': the sovereign tells us. Can you contest, or, even think this? Dare think it...there is nothing to think here; between the law and death, there is no choice, everything ends here. It is the end of the world, the end of thinking, and the end of time....In councils of Universities and in the Parliaments of the world, in the news channels and in the all powerful world of media, in stock markets and courtrooms, everywhere we daily meet the end of the world, and the end of thinking. Death, not just the death in the shape of blood-shedding of the "physical" and of the mere alive, but death which we meet in certain thoughtlessness that has become a our daily, banal reality, something that is as sinister and yet as ordinary as evil: "the banality of evil", as Hannah Arendt names it, in a strange way, that evoked more incomprehension and criticism than true understanding. It is difficult to recognize, rather it is easier to refuse to recognize that evil can be banal, as banal as cutting the head of a cabbage or swallowing a mouthful of water, as Hegel remarked once, when he tried to understand the banality of death in times of French Revolution.

What does it mean: this strange, unforgettable-unforgivable phrase—"banality of evil"? Can evil at all be banal? Do not we lovers of Bollywood cinema see our villains how grotesque and repulsive look they bear, those bulging eyes, that sinister look, that frightening voice that evoke, even more than God, "fear and trembling" in us? Such an image of evil is shattered when

Hannah Arendt saw Eichmann: an ordinary administrator whom you may meet anywhere, who thoughtlessly carries out orders that come from above, and mechanically applies rules and laws simply because they are nothing but rules and laws. "'Kill two million Jews'; 'yes sir'!" Evil is sinister-most when it is banal, imperceptible, a daily reality, like cutting the head of a cabbage and swallowing a mouthful of water. Schelling calls this evil "imbecility", thoughtlessness or inability to think that precisely is even more dangerous than those Bollywood grotesque figures. But this imbecility is not an absence of reason altogether; imbecility of this bureaucratic rationality is not what the psychiatrist would call "mad"; rather, it is precisely a specific manifestation of a reason which, nevertheless, can be altogether devoid of thinking. Schelling here critically puts into question the dominant western conception of thinking that immediately identifies it with reason. In fact, only reason in this specific manifestation can be called imbecile, stupid, or idiocy. However, there is another manifestation of stupidity or idiocy which is to be qualitatively distinguished from the imbecility mentioned above; there is another idiocy, entirely other idiocy, of Gustav Flaubert—as Jean Paul Sartre beautifully brings out for us—Flaubert who cannot even open his bedroom window. The imbecility of evil lies in its rationality that does not know what Schelling calls "ecstasy", in a specific sense. This imbecility or thoughtlessness, in utter banality and ordinariness, is thus not "madness" in simple sense of the term; it is also to be distinguished from "the divine madness" that Plato speaks of, and which in turn is called as "ecstasy" by Schelling: the divine madness out of which all the great things of Greece have come out, and all great poets and philosophers suffer from this divine madness, Socrates above all. Imbecility or this thoughtlessness is, therefore, not an innocent and impotent thing, as when we say: "oh, he is simply stupid!"; it is precisely a malicious force of a prodigious rationality, a rationality that nevertheless cannot think; or, at least it cannot in the way we are trying to understand, implicitly though, as "thinking". The most malicious evil can manifest itself to us in the most banal way possible in our everyday reality: the doting family man with whom you talk everyday over a cup of coffee; that sweet violin teacher of yours who produces the most incredible music ever; that warm and radiant friend of yours whom you invite to your house over dinner and share your costly wine; that promising young student of yours who writes beautifully and sensitively the poetry of suffering and poverty: it is she or he suddenly—under certain situation—opens his or her mouth, and utters the most dangerous thing one can hear, those words that want to murder humanity, and want to transform history into a slaughter-bench! Suddenly that lovable man, that beautiful woman, that intelligent scholar looks no less than a rioter, a terrorist, a murderer who justifies all that is unjustifiable in the name of rule, law, rationality, in a very systematically well-reasoned—like a lawyer—series of logical propositions from which so-called apodictic results are deduced! No trace of madness and absolutely no irrationality here: rationality alone is here, rationality in its utmost reduction or heightening and yet, without a single trace of thinking! It appears that certain rationality—Eichmann's rationality—is dangerous, more dangerous than any grotesque look to be read in any great gothic novels, precisely because it is banal, ordinary and common.

This dangerous "thing" called thinking

But there is also a danger of thinking. That destitute wise old man of Athens, the ugliest among the beautiful people of Greece, pot-bellied and bulging eyed, did nothing in his long life but thinking. The whole day long he keeps standing in the market place of Athens, picks up discussions with shoe-makers and poets, philosophers and tailors, asking them questions that leave them speechless. Who is poorer than Socrates, the one who does not have a pair of shoes in his feet? What is more powerless than thinking? What is more innocent and harmless than this strange thing called "thinking"? Yet, the state of Athens was scared of that poor, utterly powerless and helpless old man whose only burning passion is endless questioning! What is this power that emanates from this most destitute and powerless activity called "thinking" that makes the even the most powerful, the state with all its military and political power, tremble with fear? This enigma, this paradox of thinking which, just like love, is most powerful in-being most powerless, runs through the history of the philosophy, philosophy being, of all human discourses, is most singularly concerned with this something called "thinking"! It's not for nothing that Socrates thinks *thinking* itself in analogy with love; or, rather, thinking is *loving* itself, being the most erotic passion, as the very word *philo-sophia* bears witness. *Philo-sophia*: love of wisdom. The philosopher, then, is not the wise mortal; rather, she is the one who, lacking wisdom, is in love with *Sophia*. Like Eros whose mother is poor but whose father is rich, whose father is God but whose mother is mortal (a God who is too much of a mortal, or a mortal who has too much of divinity in him, the one who is neither mortal or human, the one in whom humanity and divinity comes to a monstrous copulation), the philosopher is neither wise nor a fool: she is then the lover par excellence. For the lover and the philosopher are analogous figures: they are rich in their poverty, and poor in their wealth. Such is the philosophical eros—the Socratic passion par excellence. And it is of this little, old, ugly, useless man of Athens that the great state of Greece is afraid! The philosopher was made to drink hemlock, and since then, till now, the philosophers are always made to drink hemlock.

So, there is a danger of thinking. Thinking is a dangerous activity. In its very fragility and destitution, thinking calls forth persecution from those institutional authorities that yield powers and forces of the law. Right from Socrates to our own time, the persecution of thinking-questioning individuals constitutes and de-constitutes the history of the human race. The very problematic place of the University, not only in today's world but always, is the emblematic example of this history: the thinkers, the intellectuals, the philosophers, the professors, the students will always be the first to be targeted and persecuted. The University, thus, has never been and will never be an idyllic, harmless, beautiful world of harmony; it is the place where bitter struggles are always fought for the freedom of the human race. For, among all institutions, the university is the philosophical institution par excellence. The very word "academy" is the Platonic one: the academy is founded by a philosopher. With philosophy, the university pursues the endless dream of a utopian cosmopolitanism, beyond all national and racial closures, from which universality the name "university" itself has come: the University pursues the universal questions of humanity, even beyond humanity, beyond all institutional closures of nationalisms. With the fate of the philosophy, it comes to be at stake the fate of the most beautiful and highest institution of humanity called "the university". Without this philosophical institution of the University which singularly pursues this unique and singular, to the point of anachronism, task of thinking, there is neither any politics nor any ethics of an intellectual existence called "thinking".

This task calls forth integrity of a certain mode of being, or certain form of life that brings together thinking and existence. Such mode of being, or such form of life is the singular cultivation of this discourse called "philosophy": 'philosophy as a way of life', as it used to be called in ancient days. Such form of life does not lie in being untouched by the mire of evil forces; it is not a beauty untouched by the forces of the negative. What we need to do today, as Walter Benjamin wrote at a time which is so uncannily similar to our demonic situation today, what we need to do is to seize or wrest away the lightning flashes of thinking that threaten to disappear in the dark abyss of the night. In other words, thinking is nothing other than an event. It is the event of making open the space of the world and the time of the world for *truth* to occur.

Does the world that we inhabit today (the world that is constantly running out of time) still have a space for the truth to occur and to welcome this event of truth? As we have seen from the history of philosophy itself, the world never has had a space for this phosphorous event of truth which suddenly erupts in the midst of beings, and makes a space for itself by a fragile and redemptive violence. And it appears that only persecuted truth can be redemptive, for they alone pose redemptive danger to the world that wants to close itself around something conditioned, while fantasizing it as the unconditional one.

The sky of eternity

But what is thinking? We are yet to see. We do not yet know. We have only been preparing ourselves to think about thinking.

The verb *penser*, derived from the Latin *penso,* means to ponder: to ponder is to weigh. What does thinking weigh? What does thinking measure? Thinking measures the immeasurable: the unthought or the unthinkable. Here lies precisely the exuberance of thinking, as both Schelling and Heidegger, in two different gestures, bring to our attention. The unthought is the origin of thinking. The origin of thinking exceeds the thinkable itself. It, then, calls for wonder or astonishment: it is towards this exuberance and un-pre-thinkable (*Unvordenkliche*, as Schelling calls it) origin that Socrates dialectically attempts to bring his interlocutors to confront. It appears as if the task of thinking lies in confronting, in marvel or in wonder, the event of the unthinkable.

The word *penser* means to weigh. The weight of thinking puts us down: this is why Auguste Rodin makes the thinker's gaze downcast. Walter Benjamin shows, in many of his short essays, how *penser* makes the thinker *pensive*: hence the melancholic gaze of the thinker with his downcast eyes! The enigmatic connection between thinking and melancholy is brought to our attention at the very inception of philosophy, by none other than Aristotle himself, in one of his famous *Problemata.* And it is the same enigma that makes Heidegger say, at the end of metaphysics, that melancholy is the fundamental attunement—the *Grundstimmung*—of thinking. This melancholy lies in the renunciation—the *Gelassenheit*—of all cognitive violence that lies in conceptual grasping and in subsuming of phenomena under the gaze of the law, with the force and power of the concept. The fundamental task of thinking, then, is none other than redemption of phenomena, to say in the unforgettable words of Walter Benjamin: to think is not the cognitive grasp of the phenomena but their salvation from violence. Bringing the proximity of the verbal resonance between *denken* and *danken*, *thinking* and *thanking*, Heidegger too shows that the task of thinking does not lie in the mythic power of the concept that grasps phenomena with the force of its subsumption, but rather, in thanks-giving, to bear witness the gift of the unthought which is the very origin of thought. Renouncing the mythic violence of the concept prepares us for the non-economy of the gift. Since in all renunciation there lies a melancholy, this melancholy attunes the Adamic language of thinking itself as its *Grundstimmung*. But this is not the oppressive melancholy that weighs us down with the threatening violence of the mythic force; it is rather the blessed sadness, the divine mournfulness where all earthly suffering is at once absorbed and redeemed. To *think* is to *thank*: *thinking* and *thanking*, *denken* and *danken*, in their very proximity, brings together an event that will one day give birth to the dancing star that will shine against the dark night in which we exist today. That is why Socrates calls the philosopher a midwife.

To be a midwife, that is to be a philosopher is to give birth to dancing stars, as Nietzsche poetized once. The weight of thinking does not merely follow the law of gravity that pulls us down. If thinking is to measure the immeasurable, and if the measure of thinking is the gift out of the abyss of the immeasurable, then this weight is also a flight and a dance and a feast of joy in the sky of eternity.

[This essay was read out as the opening remark at the conference "What is Thinking?", Jawaharlal Nehru University, November 2019].

...And this palpitation of existence

In honor of Professor Harjeet Singh Gill on his 80th birthday

Today, January 13, 2015, when we have gathered here to celebrate the 80th birthday of our beloved teacher, the beloved colleague of some us here, and the thinker whose thinking has nourished us over decades long by now and has not ceased nourishing us over all these decades too short and too long, too long being too short, I wonder: what does it mean to celebrate the birthday of someone, someone whom we admire—here someone a thinker bearing a proper name—adoring the singularity of a thought, adoring the thought of a singularity, singularity that nourishes and opens us, unceasingly, to the infinitude of a thinking? I have always thought Professor Gill as a thinker, for encountering him gives us the gift of thought, the gift of opening to the infinitude of thinking, infinitude that while departing from finitude does not leave finitude behind as left-over, infinitude enigmatic—this infinitude of thinking—that trembles, palpitates, glistens and gleams, throbs our heart in admiration. I wonder, once again, and never ceased wondering for decades long: what does it mean to think? What is this strange experience that we have learnt to call "thinking", learning without knowing or knowing without learning "anything", thinking that opens us to infinitude while never leaving finitude as mere left-over, the infinitude palpitating in the heart of finitude and is nourished on it? How to think, while thinking all along, the infinitude with finitude, this event of eternity erupting in the very midst of life while touching, at the same time, the threshold of death, touching while withdrawing, crossing over beyond while the beyond is still *the-not-yet*, the-not-yet reached and not-yet attained? How to think leaving this world while remaining in it, like a pilgrim of eternity in the desert of the world, wandering without inhabiting wherein the event of birth simultaneously touches the threshold of death, wherein all welcoming welcomes what we have not learnt, what we have not known, what we have failed to know while welcoming all along, all the while, always and ever before, immemorially? Could it be that thinking not be learnt, for it has to do with the immemorial and infinitude of an exposure to the unknown, to the unknowable that would not have to pass over into the known, which would not have to be a mere attenuated variation of the visible, which would not have to be a privation of memory and of knowledge, that which is before the memorial and visible, not in the manner of the logical "before", but in the manner in which love precedes good and evil? How is it that—so I wonder today, just like a child, just like my child—how is it that each time we welcome what is to arrive we must take leave at the same time, as though the celebration of natality, of the day that recurs every year in the calendar, is born out of mortality, out of a fragility of our existence that we know not how to name, how to know, how to remember, but may nevertheless think as something like a gift coming to us from somewhere else, from some other place, from other destination? Is thinking otherwise than this?: this gift from a destination that opens up infinitude with the palpitation of the heart, with the trembling of finitude, with the being-open of the visible? Is thinking other than always being "existential"—this being the favourite word from Professor Gill—in which we attempt to think the trembling of being, this event called "being" at all, being that can always happen otherwise than a *stasis*, otherwise than a condition presently given or an essence, otherwise than that which has come to rest in the immobility of the gaze that fixes it and knows it thus as that which is, finally, as knowable, as that which is memorisable and visible in the light of the Day? Could we, then, be able to say of the *phenomenality* of phenomenon—of this palpitation of existence—that it so *sutures* itself, exhausts itself and gives itself so completely to presence that nothing of remnant would remain, that nothing of the invisible would be able to maintain itself, that nothing which is not signification (the humming of the sea, the rustling of leaves, the murmur of the most rudimentary and elementary awakening to consciousness from the depth of slumber) would remain that is untouched by the light of the Day? Should we say of this language that is *not-yet* language, of the *potentia* of language that would not come to pass over into the immobility of a gaze, that it can be none but signification?

Re-reading some of Professor Gill's works, I am astonished by that which he wants us to hear, or rather to listen in this word, in this term or in this name, over-used by him, that is, "signification". "Structures of signification": how innumerable times will he repeat it, as though we have not yet listened to that which resonates in this word, the infinitude of verbality which overflows, exceeds, outpours the given, immobile and petrified structures of language, as though there can ever be achieved such luminosity without simultaneous darkening of the invisible, such blazing brilliance without simultaneous desertion of sense, such work of the Day without being fatigued and workless? But such failure, failure to achieve the absolute luminosity of signification, is a good thing: we learn to listen to the verbality of the infinitude that resonates in language, born out of our mortality and nourished on the fragility of existence, by having failed to achieve the immobility of the gaze that seizes, grasps and appropriates that which has *always already* de-phenomenalized itself. All those who have listened to Professor Gill—and we all know that he never says anything new but forever repeats himself—all those listeners, students and friends will remember how he evokes the distinction that Maurice Merleau-Ponty makes, that of the distinction between "thinking-thought" and "thought-thought". He then goes on to multiply examples: Michel Foucault's archaeological idea of enunciation, Mikhail Bakhtin's dialogical idea of heteroglossia, and 12th century thinker Peter Abelard's dialectical understanding of the triune God of Christianity. And we remember, in admiration, of his corrective of the translation of the title of Jean-Paul Sartre's famous book *Being and Nothingness*. He wants us to listen what Sartre listens: *to be*, that is, being in the infinitude of the verbal; and *to negate*, for the French word *néant*, in distinction from the word *rien*, implies the active verbality over the nominative. Hence we read, so Professor Gill reminds us, the title of Jean Paul Sartre's book *L'etre and le Néant*, "to be and to negate". I would like to supplement Professor Gill here by a short discussion of the famous letter on humanism wherein Martin Heidegger criticizes Sartre's existentialism, Heidegger listens to Sartre's insistence on the verbality of the infinitude of this *néant* in a manner that many of the professed Sartre's disciples do not listen to, for this term or the word *néant* has a conceptual history that Sartre himself traces back to what Hegel means by the word *Negation* in all its *inquietitude*, in all the restless energy with which the concept unleashes the movement of history. It is another matter that it is the same Hegel in the same book called *Phenomenology of Spirit* summons up the "patience of the spirit" that abides, makes itself an abode, by letting what comes to pass. Could it that the inquietitude of existence—so tied up with the impatience of language, this palpitation of being—be heard or listened to in the dialectical movement without being absorbed into the totality which this movement constantly pre-supposes? I remember in a certain text that reads Jean-Paul Sartre, Professor Gill is attentive (which shows what a great scholar we have amongst us) to the notion of totality implied therein, an attention that brings a tension in Professor Gill's own works, an unbearable tension between the notion of *totality* and the structure of signification which we can arrive at by showing conceptual pairs of opposition and, on the other hand, the event of being that would not rest exhausted in any given totality, an event which Professor Gill himself names (and what a beautiful name it is!) as "existential", this incessant palpitation of being, this trembling not yet at rest and is still trembling, trembling without reaching stillness, without reaching the patience of the concept. Existence: outside, ex- of insistence and persistence, without respite! Some of the medieval apocalyptic writers, especially Joachim of Fiore from 12th century, ask us to listen to this verbality in the word they use: *transire.* Thus when Martin Heidegger uses the word *transcendenz* in his *Sein und Zeit*, we must listen to the resonance of the infinitude of the verbal: it is the essence of *Existenz* that the-there (Da- of *Da-sein*) always *transcends*, in such a way that we must understand the title *Sein und Zeit* as "*to* be and *to* time", for it is not time as such (the nominative-entitative) that interests Heidegger but *to time* (the verbal), in the same way that it is not being (entitative-nominative) that interests Heidegger but always *to be* (the verbal infinity), that is, its eruption from the *Abgrund*, from-without-ground, of mortality *towards* which it goes ahead, this "towards" implying the innermost transcendence of existence. Heidegger's existential analytic of *Dasein* listens to the verbal resonance of being-*there* in its "to" and "towardness", a going ahead a *toward* that which *arrives* from the futurity, as though from the extremity of time.

During all these years since I met Professor Gill for the first time—I still remember that day—it is his speaking of the word *existential* that has always fascinated me more than those other words which are generally associated with him, those now well-known words that we have learnt to speak with him and from him to speak that which comes to us as an event of thought, to speak of "structure", of "signification", of "semiotics" etc. And as I write the word *existential*, I can now almost hear the breath that emanates from his voice and listen to the singular intensity that his voice lends to the word as he utters it: *existential*! For long have I associated the name, the proper name Harjeet Singh Gill with this breath, this breath almost imperceptible, passing through this indiscernible passage between the concept and phenomenon, passing without being *passé* and thus is always arriving as the event which, for me, is not yet signification, which *spaces* a space *still available* and *times* a time *still remaining*: so I utter, with him, from him–"existence", the-there of the outside that happens, arrives and comes, and that is always new for me, while uttering the same word with him, always the same word. And we know Professor Gill utters only a few words, the same words for all these decades, always the same words, words that are yet always new, renewed in contemplation: "structure", "semiotics", "signification", "existence", "table", "chair", "father", "son", "nominalism", "realism". If you search, you may perhaps find one or two more words, but nothing more. Where, then—so we wonder—is this event of language to be heard? Professor Gill, who is trained in linguistics and semiotics in his youth, answers: it is neither in the predicative structure of logical proposition, nor in the syntactic-morpho-phonological structures of supposedly universal language. Where, then, is this event of language to be heard? He comes to answer, more decisively in these last few years of his life: it is in the language of poetry and in the language of art, and even in the language of translation, is there to be heard the resonance of the verbal infinitude of language, of language in its palpitation and trembling, of language in its and as its *existential*, in the linguistic trembling of existence, or even better, in the *existential* palpitation of language. In poetic language and in language of art there opens up the Open where language happens, arrives and comes. In poetry and in art, language *as such* trembles. I said "as such". This is not a phrase that he ever uses, but it is all there. One has to read him in spirit and not just in its letter.

Here is an instance of this trembling, of this palpitation, of the beating of the heart, of life persisting and still persisting while it is in suspension, of existence suspending in tumultuous voluptuousness. Professor Gill is reading here Gustav Flaubert. He is reading Flaubert's incomparable *Saint Julien*. He criticises the great translator Robert Baldick of Oxford University for not listening to this palpitation of existence, this beating of the heart, this heart of language that beats and is still beating in savage and tumultuous voluptuousness. How can a translator not listen to the heart of language? Is it not the task of the translator to listen to the heart of language, to welcome the arrival of language, to welcome so that language may come *to* itself in the Open of existence? Here is the French paragraph:

> Le pigeon, les ailes cassés, palpitait, suspendu dans les branches d'un troène. La persistence de sa vie irrita l'enfant. Il se mit à l'étrangler; et les convulsions de l'oiseau faisaient battre son coeur, l'emplissaient d'une volupté sauvage et tumultueuse. Au dernier raidissement, il se sentit défaillir...

Here is the translation by Robert Baldick:

> The pigeon, its wings broken and its body quivering, was caught in the branches of a privet. Its stubborn refusal to die infuriated the child. He set about wringing its neck, and its convulsions made his heart beat wildly, filling him with a savage, passionate delight. When it finally went still in his hands he felt he was going to faint...

Professor Gill now comments. Let us now listen to him listening, let us listen with him listening—to this palpitation of existence, to this throbbing of the heart and to the savage and tumultuous voluptuousness:

> *This passage shows most clearly what indeed has gone wrong in this rendering. A highly internalised existential situation has been transformed into an extrovert state, inflicting a major psychic deviation on the kernel theme of this discourse of St. Julien. The "palpitating" (heart) is rendered as "quivering body", and "suspension" is taken as "caught". It is interesting to note that throughout the English translation, the "movement" is rendered as a static state. "The persistence of its life" is somehow understood as "its stubborn refusal to die" and "irrita l'enfant" becomes "infuriated the child". The persistence of life is an internal affair, a state of hyper-*

> *tension from within as is the notion of "irritation". Both of these concepts are interrelated and lead to a unified psychic interpolation. On the other hand, the stubborn refusal to die and the infuriated state point to a conscious act, an external behaviour, almost an outburst, a state of mind most unfamiliar to Julien. This English rendering demonstrates a complete misunderstanding of the discourse of St. Julien. "The convulsions of the bird made his heart beat" has becomes "its convulsions made his heart beat wildly". Why this addition of "wildly"? And, the translation goes on with "filling him with a savage, passionate delight" where the French version refers to a "volupté sauvage et tumultueuse". How on earth can one equate "savage and tumultuous voluptuousness" with "savage and passionate delight"? Passionate delight and tumultuous voluptuousness refer to two very different psychic centres of external and internal mental states. There is no question of a passionate delight, there is within the innermost layers of Julien's mind, a state of tumultuous upheaval which makes him feel "défaillir", disintegrate, decompose, faint. It is only from a storm within that one disintegrates, and not from a state of passionate delight.* (Gill 1991: 640).

This passage all throughout is italicized. I do not know a better way to celebrate the 80th birthday of my beloved teacher than to listen to him once more and always once more—to this palpitation of existence!

REFERENCES

Gill, Harjeet Singh, "Semiotic Analysis of a Literary Text: La Légende de Saint Julien L' Hopitalier of Gustav Flaubert: Method and Praxis" in *Journal of the School of Languages,* Vol. III ("Structures of Signification"), (New Delhi: Jawaharlal Nehru University, 1991).

When religion has (not) returned?

It is said these days—and this is soon becoming a grand narrative in our time—that there is a return of religion. Religion is supposed to have gone somewhere, disappeared mysteriously one day, and has now returned in full health: some congratulate this return; others lament and ascribe all possible evils of our contemporary civilization—genocide, religious war, communal violence, religious fundamentalism, etc.—to this supposed return of religion. These are good "secularists" who think the very word "secularism" itself—whatever that means hardly one bothers to investigate—smells good, and everything secular is progressive, an idea built upon the 18th and 19th century ideology of progress. Very few people are interested to inquire how and when this ideology of progress emerged, as if secularism is an ahistorical category, and has by nature in it something good, glorious and that serves the best interest of mankind, as opposed to religion that smells all that is inglorious, superstitious, fanaticism and obscurantism. All that is evil can now be traced back to this origin. This supposed return of religion in our contemporary civilization has supposed to have brought back all the elements of the night—chthonic, elemental, dark and primeval—which are better to remain repressed and buried under the earth.

When has, or better, when has not religion returned, supposing it has returned, having gone by one day, a return marked by the scandal that religion itself is supposed to be (oh, this the eternal scandal of humanity!)? Does not the word "religion"—*re-ligio*— in its very etymological origin, mean return, turning again and again to the *bond* to which one is avowed? The very essence of religion itself would then be that it returns, that it always returns, and has never ceased returning from its inception whose moment we cannot decipher or locate in the history of humanity. This would precisely mean—and this is the strange contradiction— that the diagnosis according to our grand narrative, that there is "now" a return of religion, is not really true, precisely because not only "now"—today and here—but always religion returns: it is destined to return according to its very destiny, sense and meaning. This "now" of return loses its uniqueness in the vast, anonymous, indifferential sea of "always". When, then, religion has returned and why religion has to return? Or better, taking a step back, when has religion ever gone from the history of the human race? Or, may be instead of religion having gone, it is rather that our relation with religion has undergone a certain transmutation or transformation, and that religion appears to have lost something of its sense of ultimate horizon of meaning for us? Not disappearance, but somewhat like an "exit" of *certain* absolute—one should emphasize the word "certain" here— from the horizon of our historical meaning. It would be too presumptuous from here to suppose that absolute *as such* has exited, for supplements or substitutes for the lost absolute always arrive in full abundance: they vie with each other to replace itself as the new absolute. The exit of religion may be, then, the exit of a certain absolute, but not absolute as such. This is, then, the first thing we have learnt from the exit of religion: that religion is not the—and the only—absolute.

What is called "secularism" or "secularizing" is this exit of religion from the horizon of ultimate meaning, and we will see soon that it means something much more than this. At a certain historical epoch, or rather, as certain event of epochal transformation in the West, secularization has come into being. What we generally mean by "secularism" in Indian discursive contexts is actually something entirely different from what secularizing actually meant, which is a historical process that has made itself into an event of epochal transformation. Secularism as this event of epochal transformation does not mean what we generally understand by it: as tolerating many religious practices to co-exist, and to be able to arrive at political or public policies for common public existence which are relatively neutral to specific religious practices. The word "secular" comes from the Latin *Saeculum*, which means "worldly". In Saint Augustine, *saeculum* is that mode of being on this earthly or worldly city, as against the *cité de deo*, the city of God (Markus 1989). To *secularize*—in the verbal sense—is to translate, by a displacement of meaning, transcendence into immanence. This has the meaning, from which certain violence—a metaphysical violence—is inseparable, of dethroning transcendence as the origin and the legitimating principle of worldly-political existence. At stake here, then, is the immense theologico-political significance: the theological can no longer claim to have the political significance of legitimation. The new legitimating principle is Reason, the principle of immanence par excellence: as the principle of all authority, Reason alone supplies the hegemonic fantasm of the modern epoch. In the name of Reason, which Immanuel Kant famously calls the principle of "autonomy" in his well known essay on Enlightenment, man gives himself the self-justified right to govern himself: *auto-nomos*—the law of the *auto*, or self-legitimation—in the name of which all *hetero-nomos* (God or nature) are to be excluded, repressed, or abandoned (Kant 1999: 11-22).

At the heart of this problematic lies the question of "legitimation". Dethroning of God or nature as the legitimating principle of the intra-mundane worldly existence does not mean de-legitimation of any *arché* or principle as such. The displacement of any *hetero-nomos*—whether that is understood as the law of

God or the law of nature—does not mean doing away with *nomos* itself. It rather means replacement or substitution of a new *nomos*, a new mode of legitimation, a new fantasm constituting a new epochal hegemony which we would call "modernity". The epochal condition of modernity is grounded or principled on a new sovereign fantasm: the self-legitimating Subject, the auto-generating and autonomous, and the autochthonic-autarchic authority that does not need any transcendental ground for it to exist. The immanence of this self-presence—of the sovereign Subject—is then shown to be processual and progressive: this is the great contribution of Hegel's metaphysics of history. What we can truly call a "theodicy"—in fact, this is Hegel's own use of the word "theodicy"—Hegel's metaphysics of history shows Being as essentially a historical Subject: the Subject that, with its "cunning of reason", realizes itself progressively on the linear scale of historical time (Hegel 1900). Hegel here *secularizes* the Judeo-Christian notion of eschatological time, and transforms the theological idea of *salvation history* into the world-historical plane of the Subject's self-realization (Löwith 1957). What, then, is truly meant by secularization is specifically this event: the translation, which is also transformation, of the theological-eschatological notion of *salvation history* into an intra-mundane worldly process. The divine *oikonomia* of God's self-manifestation is now transformed into a dialectical-phenomenological manifestation of the Subject as the Subject of world-historical becoming. The logic of revelation, whose secret God alone knows, has now become the truth of the Subject. Hegel's philosophy of religion or, rather, his theodicy is an atheistic transformation of the Christian Trinitarian eschatology: the Trinity becomes the world historical-political teleology. The concept or, the ideology of progress is the product of this secularization process, the idea that humanity, as this world-historical Subject, is constantly progressing, and is thus progressive, and this process is a progressive doing away of everything that is heteronymous, whether that be God or nature. Everything that is heterological to this self-legislative Reason is considered to be irrational, superstitious, obscurantist and fanatic: Reason here opposes itself to what it itself names as "religion". The self-legitimation of the autonomous Subject is the self-positing of certain sovereignty. It gives itself the sovereign lordship over all beings, even over God or nature. The Subject does not need anymore any transcendental ground to legitimate its hegemony over all other beings.

At stake here, in this problematic of secularism, is the question of man's positing and instituting itself as auto-legislative and auto-legitimate authority among all beings on earth; and not only on earth, it extends even to planetary domination under the apparatus of technology in today's world. In the absence of a transcendental-eschatological judgment on history (on the violence of history), history becomes the all pervasive and all tyrannical order of totality. The human is no longer afraid of the apocalyptic judgment that will put into question the incalculable violence that erupts from her sovereign exercise of power over nature, over all beings on earth, and even over God himself. For the human does not have, within her possession, the measure to measure out the danger of her abyssal freedom: she herself is measured by an immeasurable measure of freedom which exceeds her, because it, first of all, opens her to herself. This is the essential opening of being to Being as such (as Martin Heidegger would like to say) out of the abyss of freedom. In the epochal condition of modernity which as we have seen to be a secularizing theodicy of history—where all that is transcendence, God or nature, is thrown to the wind—immanence has become tyrannical, for there is no eschatological judgment upon the violence of history anymore; and in this way this immanence itself has become like the old, legitimating principle of transcendence, the ground of all authority and power. In today's world, nothing is more absent than God: God has absconded, fled, from the earthly being of the world (*Deo Absconditus*!). What mostly exists today as religion as one among other institutions of the worldly existence, is nothing other than a secular institution like any other institutions: it serves the legitimacy-seeking world-political powers, unless we release the understanding of religion itself from such narrow determination of it, and understand it in a more originary manner: as affirmation of infinity, or of transcendence that puts all legitimation of worldly powers into question. In fact, this is the theologico-political teaching of the Pauline letters in the New Testament: eschatologically understood, religion is the *kenotic* emptying out of all worldly powers, as St Paul speaks of it in his letter to the Philippians 2:7.

The violence of history in this epochal condition of modernity exceeds all possible violence that existed in other epochs, not just the violence that lies in the physical extinction of an individual, or even in the possible extinction of the human race altogether in today's world of atomic bomb, but also in the violence against nature, leading to incalculable and no more reparable ecological crisis, and in the large scale, immeasurable depletion of living as such. We do not need to give too obvious examples of the colonial violence, of the immeasurable horrors of two world wars, countless genocides and destruction of millions of Jews, etc. The human's sovereign claims over all that is earthly, and his deification of intra-mundane existence as the sole legitimate mode of existence in the world in the narcissistic age of secular mass consumption: this is impossible without its support on the sole sovereign fantasm of the modern hegemony—the Subject as the *auto-nomos*!

That Hegel's theodicy of immanence is a new legitimation of sovereignty: this is the critique that Marx and Nietzsche, on one hand, atheistically offer; and on the other, Kierkegaard offers in the name of Christian faith. Despite Marx's claim that he could make Hegel walk on feet again, the Hegelian secular-atheistic transformation of an apocalyptic eschatology into teleology of world-historical becoming remains the driving force of Marx's own revolutionary vision of history. As opposed to Marx, in a counter-communist manifesto manner, Kierkegaard eschatologically-Christianly opposes all possible theodicy on the plane of worldly existence (Löwith 1991), and thereby decisively breaks away from the epochal condition of modernity, and from the secularizing process of self-legislating Reason that has now been transformed into instrumental rationality, based upon the teleological ideology of progress. Kierkegaard's, and also Nietzsche's critiques, in two opposing ways, of the ideology of progress underlying the secularizing project of modernity lie in their critique of politics, of European politics, that was newly emerging that time, and whose heirs we are, the politics that we call now "democracy". It is Kierkegaard, already few years before Nietzsche, who effectively demonstrates the fundamental contradiction of all modern, secular-liberal democracy: democracy is that hegemonic regime where *demos* is missing; that what we call "public" is a fantasm, an anonymous entity—no one and everyone—a fictive entity, ideologically shaped and produced by the all powerful apparatus of media; that modern secular-democracy is inseparable from certain potential totalitarianism whose fecundity is the massification of narcissistic individuals, and the violent reduction of singular beings into homogenous, quantifiable, universal categories; and that this totalizing character of modern state has to do with the liquidification and neutralization, not only of the eschatological character of the religious but also of that irreducible, existential mode of singular being. Existence cannot be reduced to the anonymous system of knowledge (Kierkegaard 2009). The incorporation and integration of individuals under the totalizing form of the universal: this is the essence of totalitarianism that we have seen realized in the first half of the 20th century, and it is already prognosticated and diagnosed by Kierkegaard and Nietzsche, in entirely two different ways. Instead of "one"—the *mono* of monarchy—now we have a fantastic, anonymous, faceless entity called the *demos* which is supposed to rule in democracies, which in actuality does not exist as a responsible, political subject. With the loss of transcendence, legitimacy as such has not disappeared; it has now merely been replaced by a new, so called secular, entity, a hegemonic fantasm called "the public".

What Kierkegaard's—and also Nietzsche's—critique of European politics shows is that it is not enough to replace one hegemonic legitimacy with another, to replace one *arché* with a new one. The so-called secularized ideology of progress of the 19th century does exactly that, an ideology whose heir we are. This secularization is none other than secularization *of* the theological wherein the whole apocalyptic sting of eschatological judgment is neutralized. The result, as we have seen in Hegel's metaphysics of history, is the deification of the profane order of worldly powers. The modern state of Prussia, thus, becomes for Hegel a figure of the Absolute, the objective expression of the Absolute Spirit. Here is the apology of the world at the highest metaphysical level.

In his 1922 book called *Political Theology*, Carl Schmitt (Schmitt 2005) demonstrates that most significant political concepts in our contemporary thought are secularization *of* the theological concepts: thus, the idea of exception is analogous with the idea of miracle. This analogy between the theological and the political is constitutive of what Carl Schmitt names as "political theology". Against the secularizing neutralization of politics in the liberal-parliamentary democracy, Carl Schmitt raises the necessity of the apocalyptic transcendence—the very place of exception in regard to the normative order of legality—transcendence which is liquidified in the pantheistic metaphysics of immanence of 19th century, above all in Hegelian theodicy. According to Schmitt, Hegel's pantheistic metaphysics of history, which is the secularization of the theological, makes impossible conceiving of *auctoritus*, consequently making it impossible the very place of politics. Only by re-introducing the theological—that means the apocalyptic elements—into the political domain can sovereignty is possible to be thought. Schmitt's political theology is, then, a kind of apocalyptic counter-revolutionary thinking. One way to understand, then, what we mean by "return of religion" is in this sense: re-introducing the apocalyptic elements into the political, to make possible thereby the place of legitimacy as exception to the normative order of legality without which, so Schmitt argues, there is no politics. Schmitt thereby puts into question the neat distinction that liberal-secular thought introduces between the public and the private, between the political space and the apolitical; for the liberal-secular thought supposes as if there can be a space that is inviolable to politics, untouched by the political. Schmitt thereby makes politics total: there is nothing outside politics, for even apolitical is also the political gesture par excellence. Therefore, it is not for nothing that Schmitt's conservative apocalyptic counter-revolutionary thinking can fascinate the Marxist thinkers: against the liberal-secular neutralization of politics, Schmitt provides a theological foundation of politics that would be called "political theology".

At stake, in Schmitt's political theology, is the question of sovereignty as *raison d'état*. In exceptional situation when the chaos rises up from below, threatening the order of the state, decision is made necessary which is the prerogative only of the sovereign figure, the sovereign being he who makes decision at the state of exception. Schmitt's political theology is, then, the legitimization of sovereignty on a theological foundation: what God is above, the sovereign is below—indivisible, solitary, exception to the order that he founds. The normative-legal order is suspended at the state of exception in order to preserve the state: this non-identity between the legal order and the legitimizing sovereignty is crucial to understand why, for Schmitt, the concept of transcendence is a necessary one.

The immense political consequences that may arise from such a political theology were already concretely visible after few years of publication of Schmitt's text. At the exceptional situation of civil uprising in Germany in the third decade of the last century, Schmitt comes justify the dictatorship of Hitler by using a certain Article from the constitution which grants exceptional power to the dictator to suspend the basic constitutional rights altogether. The result is for everyone to see: with the rise of Hitler, there was the murder of six million Jews, and the unspeakable horrors of the Second World War.

The return of the apocalyptic elements, then, needs to be welcomed in a different way: not as providing the theological foundation of worldly sovereignty, but rather as eschatological suspension of *nomos* and of all worldly sovereignty. Such is the negative political theology that Carl Schmitt's adversary Jacob Taubes offers (Taubes 2003). Here the political theology is not apocalyptic in a counter-revolutionary way of serving the *raison d'état* but that of messianic de-legitimation of all worldly sovereignty on any theological foundation. It is, then, necessary—if political theology is not to serve as apology of worldly powers—to separate the theological and the political, not in the manner of the secularizing neutralization of the theological, but as the messianic or eschatological de-legitimation of all worldly powers. The negative political theology is a messianic turning antinomic; it is an eschatological refusal to recognize in the world-political figure of sovereignty our ultimate normative obligation. The eschatological or the messianic element is indeed exception to the normative order of *nomos*, but this exception does not function as legitimating principle of sovereignty. In other words, we can call this negative political theology of exception as exception without sovereignty.

It is in the theologico-political works of Walter Benjamin we find expressed such a negative political theology of exception without sovereignty. In his cryptic *Theologico-Political Fragment*, written in an uncertain year, Walter Benjamin conceives of a pure politics of nihilism: the worldly existence belongs to the order of 'passing away', 'transient in its totality', 'for nature is Messianic by reason of its eternal and total passing away. To strive after such passing, even for those stages of man that are nature, is the task of world politics, whose method must be called nihilism' (Benjamin 1986: 313). The idea of the worldly order as transient is resonant here with the Pauline spirit: the task of politics, the politics of pure means, is that of *kenosis*—the emptying out of all worldly attributes of sovereignty. This messianic *kenosis* of the worldly order destitutes all worldly hegemonies. Early in the fragment,

Benjamin opposes such messianic establishment of the divine Kingdom against 'the *telos* of the historical dynamic':

> Only the Messiah himself consummates all history, in the sense that he alone redeems, completes, creates its relation to the Messianic. For this reason nothing historical can relate itself on its own account to anything Messianic. Therefore the Kingdom of God is not the *telos* of the historical dynamic; it cannot be set as a goal. From the standpoint of history it is not the goal, but the end. Therefore the order of the profane cannot be built up on the idea of the Divine Kingdom, and therefore theocracy has no political, but only a religious meaning'. (Ibid: 312).

In this opposition of the messianic to the historical dynamic, and the messianic consummation as the end to the *telos* of historical Reason, Benjamin puts into question the whole ideology of progress that underlies the immanent metaphysics of history of modernity. The messianic idea of redemption cannot be understood at the level of world-historical politics: in other words, 'theocracy has no political, but only a religious meaning'. This distinction between the religious and the political makes all attempts at embodiment of the divine at the level of world-historical reality questionable. The Hegelian theodicy of history, which is the secularization of the Judeo-Christian eschatological thought, is put into question by Benjaminian messianism: the messianic kingdom is not automatically realized in a progressive manner on the immanent plane of 'homogenous, empty time'; the messianic is rather the transcendence breaking through, and breaking apart the continuum plane of worldly existence, making the worldly existence pass away. The messianic event is an exception (not the exception that founds any earthly sovereignty) that which unfounds world-historical regimes and de-legitimates them.

In his *Theses on the Philosophy of History* (Benjamin 1985: 253-64), this exception turns itself against the Schmittean political theology of sovereignty. Thus, in the thesis VIII we read the following:

> The tradition of the oppressed teaches us that the "state of emergency" in which we live is not the exception but the rule. We must attain to a conception of history that is in keeping with this insight. Then we shall clearly realize that it is our task to bring about a real state of emergency, and this will improve our position in the struggle against Fascism (Ibid: 257).

The state of exception, as Schmitt conceives, becomes a rule in turn. What we need is a real state of exception that does not become rule in turn. Benjamin conceives of such a real state of exception as dialectical image that radically ruptures the immanent plane of the world-historical progress, and brings about something absolutely heterogeneous and new.

We may, then, understand the so-called "return of religion" in still another way: the eschatological or messianic de-legitimation of worldly hegemonies, which means, de-legitimation of any attempt to found worldly politics of sovereignty on any theological foundation. In this sense, "religion" is to be understood in an entirely heterogeneous way, in a way which is decidedly opposed and irreducible to what we generally understand by "religion". Keeping Benjamin's and Bloch's views in mind—that theocracy has no political, but only religious meaning—theocracy, in true sense, does not refer to world-political regimes on theological foundation as opposed to secular democracies. Any world-political regime of sovereignty by an appeal to the theological foundation is also, and only, a secular institution, like any other secular-worldly institutions, and can have only political meaning. This means, this neat opposition—which is normative in so-called progressive-liberal political discourses prevalent today—the opposition between so-called theocracy (world-political regime founded on theological justification) and secular-liberal democracy is a false one, not merely in the sense that—as Schmitt reminds us—the significant political concepts are of theological in origin. The so-called return of religion, then, in true sense of the term, is not to be understood as those political uses of sovereign violence by an appeal to religious foundation—as in fanaticism and fundamentalism growing in today's world like mushroom after the rain—but to be understood as *opening* or *spacing* open an *outside* of the totalization and totalitarianism of politics, an outside of the world, not to another world as opposed to *this* world, but outside of the world *as such*. It is this *outside*—the non-totalizable—that the messianic or eschatological affirms. It affirms this outside by interrupting, or arresting the continuous march of world-historical Reason by *setting apart* the world from its very foundation. *The holy* means, as Jacob Taubes points out, *separation* and *setting apart*; the holy interrupts the mythic foundation of the world (Taubes 2009: 194).

"Re" of religion, is not to be understood as return to the same and to the autarchic, to the aboriginal and autochthonous: such return to the same is to be understood as "mythic". Thus, when Carl Schmitt says that to the great politics belongs the *arcanum* (Schmitt 1996: 34), the meaning of the *arcanum* is here the mythic: for Carl Schmitt, politics is mythically founded. Against the mythic foundation of all worldly hegemonies, and all its mythic violence, Benjamin opposes the divine or the messianic (Benjamin 1986: 277-300). What returns in *re-ligio* is the bond or covenant with the divine or the messianic that returns to explode the world from its foundation rather than any returning to a mythic foundation. Any worldly political regimes of sovereignty on so-called theological foundation are actually founded on a mythic foundation. The divine, or the messianic, on the other hand, suspends and explodes any such mythic constitution of worldly regimes. The violence that accompanies such suspension—suspension of all mythic violence—is rightly called by Benjamin as *divine violence*. It is a paradoxical violence, in so far as it arrests all violence that erupts from mythic foundation, and as such, it must be violence without violence. The mythic violence is bloody; the divine violence is 'lethal without spilling blood'; 'mythical violence is bloody power over mere life for its own sake, divine violence pure power over all life for the sake of the living' (Ibid: 297).

[This paper was read out as the inaugural address at the conference on *Religion in Cultural and Comparative Perspective*, organised by the Department of Comparative Literature, Hyderabad Central University, February 2019]

REFERENCES

Benjamin, Walter, *Reflections*, trans. Peter Demetz (New York: Schocken Books, 1986).

Benjamin, Walter, "Theses on the Philosophy of History" in *Illuminations*, trans. Harry Zohn (New York: Schocken Books, 1985), 253-64.

Hegel, G.W.F., *Lectures On the Philosophy of History*, trans. J. Sibree (London: G. Bells & Sons, 1900).

Kant, Immanuel, "An Answer to the Question: What is Enlightenment?" in *Practical Philosophy*, trans. Mary Gregor (Cambridge: Cambridge University Press, 1999), 11-22.

Kierkegaard, Søren, *Two Ages*, trans. Howard Hong & Edna Hong (Princeton: Princeton University Press, 2009).

Löwith, Karl, *From Hegel to Nietzsche: The Revolution in the Nineteenth Century Thought,* trans. David E. Green (New York: Columbia University Press, 1991).

Löwith, Karl, *The Meaning of History The Theological Implication of the Philosophy of History* (Chicago: Chicago University Press, 1957).

Markus, R.A., *Saeculum: History and Society in the Theology of St. Augustine* (Cambridge: Cambridge University Press, 1989).

Schmitt, Carl, *Political Theology: Four Chapters on the Concept of Sovereignty*, trans. George Schwab (Chicago: Chicago University Press, 2005).

Schmitt, Carl, *Roman Catholicism and Political Form*, trans. G.L. Ulmen (New York: Greenwood Press, 1996).

Taubes, Jacob, *Occidental Eschatology*, trans. David Ratmoko (Stanford: Stanford University Press, 2009).

Taubes, Jacob, *The Political Theology of Paul*, trans. Dana Hollander (Stanford: Stanford University Press, 2003).

(Dis)Figures of death

Taking the side of Derrida, taking the side of death

If the dominant ethico-philosophical thinking of responsibility in the West is founded upon, or tied to a certain figure of death, it is because this ethical notion of responsibility is also a certain econo-onto-thanatology. Here the notion of the gift to the other is *always already* inscribed within a certain economic equivalence of value, or an economic determination of temporality as the geometric figure of the circle, or a certain economy of the experiences of abandonment and mourning, through which the event-character of the gift, its excess and its infinite surplus is economized, reduced, repressed, or even annulled. Reading Jacques Derrida's deconstruction of this econo-onto-thanatology, and relating him to Schelling, Heidegger, Levinas and Kierkegaard, this article attempts to reveal this very complex relationship of the ethical notion of responsibility and the gift with death, in order to think anew—in the spirit of Derrida—a responsibility in relation to mourning and abandonment, and in relation to a death that does not figure in any figuration of self-figuration and self-presence, but—to speak with Maurice Blanchot—as interminable, incessant worklessness, as endless ruination and abandonment of itself. This impossible aporia of the notion of responsibility is itself a dis-figuring of death, which is also an aporia of an instant which escapes, in its event character, the geometric figure of time as circle.

*

DYING—
Awaiting (one another at) The 'limits of truth'
MOURIR—
s'attendre aux 'limites de la vérité'
—Derrida 1993, epigraph

The patience of time

So Derrida (2006) says, towards the end of his life, responding to his lifelong friend Helen Cixous that, contrary to her taking side of life, it is to death that he always has had a feeling of being drawn to, as if one whose proper name is 'Derrida', is already anticipating, awaiting, at the limit of 'truth', at the edge of the world, at the 'border' of a seashore for what is still remaining, what is *to come*. Dying, inseparable from this awaiting one another, is always a question of the 'limit', of the 'border', of the 'threshold' that separates one another, one from another, one from oneself; and above all, it is the question of a (non)relation to that which is yet *to come*, to what has remained, to what is a remainder, the remnant of an *arrival*. To be drawn to death is to endure this awaiting in its not being able to endure this 'patience and length of time'[1]—in Levinas' felicitous phrase (Levinas 2000: 7-8)—which is always an awaiting in mourning, as if awaiting itself *as such* has something to do with an (non)experience of mourning. To await one another at 'the limit of truth' is to endure the 'patience and length of time' (Levinas 2000: 7-8) where grief watches us, where grief watches every word that we write for one another. Who more than Blanchot has written for us, in that strange trembling writing that is uniquely and singularly his, of this strange relation of writing with mourning, with grief, and above all with dying and disappearing, and also with awaiting at 'the limit of truth'?

Strange limit it is, an impossible threshold: of absence-presence, neither one nor the other, but a passivity, a non-power and a non-capacity which Blanchot in his long complaint against Heidegger, calls 'impossibility of all possibilities' (Blanchot 1995: 70). Is it not that Derrida calls *trace*? Trace: the word that he borrows from Levinas to speak of the trace of writing, or better, writing as trace, which insofar as it is awaiting for what is *to* arrive, is *already always* its own erasure. Hence is this mourning, this not-being-able to assume the origin of oneself, not-to-be-able-to be there at the origin, so that *already always* a *differance*, pre-originary—in relation to myself, in relation to my 'own' death—that has made the origin a *prosthesis,* so that all monolingualism is *always already* the language of the other, so that awaiting for oneself is *always already* awaiting for the other, no longer 'my' death as properly 'mine' as authentic, *Eigentlich*, but awaiting in mourning at the 'limit' of truth.[2] To respond to the other who is to come—writing is the site of responsibility to the other, in so far as in writing 'I' disappears and the other arrives—is not to respond to the other out of duty [as Kant suggests in his *Groundwork of the Metaphysics of Morals* (1996)], nor to assume responsibility out of my *power*, my *capacity*, my *possibility* to assume decision and responsibility, but precisely as non-power, non-capacity, non-possibility of an infinite mourning which is an excess of the Idea, even of the regulative Idea (and not constitutive or theoretical), even if it not founded upon a Speculative reason of duty and morality, of universal morality and ethics.

Yet, is it not that the very idea of responsibility demands the idea of duty and obligation, of being able to assume decision and responsibility in the face of my irreplaceable death precisely in order to respond to the other's death, since in my death—so Heidegger insists—only I die? I cannot assume the other's death, for each one dies one's own death; I cannot die *in the place* of the other, though I can die *for* the other, which is the dying of my death *for* the other without replacing her death. Is not this very non-place of death, this not—being-able-to die *in the place of* the other, precisely the condition of the possibility of responsibility for the other's death, of my being able to die *for* the other? As if this aporia marks the very idea of responsibility an impossible idea. It is an aporia between *possible* and *impossible*, or, to complicate the problem more, between the 'possibility of all impossibilities' and 'the impossibility of all possibilities' of death, which is the 'possibility of all impossibilities' and 'impossibility of all possibilities'.

It is this aporia of responsibility, which is the very (dis)figure of death, thanks to Derrida, that Derrida brings to our notice: the aporia, on the one hand, of the demand of a philosophical foundation of an ethics to think of responsibility at all, *as such*, even as a conceivable, thinkable idea at all, and on the other hand, a responsibility outside all foundation of a philosophical ethics, outside even anything like conceivable, or thinkable *as such*, even outside any responsible idea of responsibility in the name of a responsibility which, like death, is outside of all names. It is, like death, secret.

The proper name

To take the side of death, to take the side of aporia: is not aporia the very (dis)figure, in so far as it does not figure itself *as* the figure of death? Is not this very figure of aporia an aporetic, an impossible experience of mourning *as such*? What is the relation, or the connection between, let us say, the very *figurality* of figure, and mourning as *figuration* (or, rather *disfiguration*), of which mourning that we (or, rather Derrida) evokes here? To take the side of death: of which death and of which mourning? Is it the death of the one who has learnt how to die, who through this exercise and learning has learnt to-be-beside oneself at the event of death, so that at the moment of that absolute separation there is also the utmost proximity, of self to self, the utmost opening of self *to* itself (in the infinitude of the verbal resonance 'to')? Is it rather the other 'one' whom death takes (a)side, the other 'one' who is *always already* unlearnt by an excessive mourning, a mourning that has refused to be inscribed in the interiority of a self to gather oneself to oneself at the very limit of its possibility, a mourning that has refused to be an inscription (in the sense of allowing a hermeneutic reading of this inscription to be possible, or even a psycho-analytic one), a mourning that has *always already* rendered impossible to constitute oneself to be a self as a result of a process of subjectification? Or rather death takes the side of the 'one' who could not be a being among beings of the world, but whom mourning has her cast apart from the world, made her a stranger to the world, whose proper name signifies to the world that absolutely singular and absolutely irreplaceable, that unique individual with a proper name, which has become for this unique individual the name of a non-propriety and non-proper-ness[3], in the sense that she could not make her death as her death, death that ought to have been her authentic death, her very proper death, her very own death. Is it not this authenticity (*Eigentlichkeit*) that concerns us—as Heidegger reminds us—in our very 'being-towards-death', our care (*Sorge*) for the facticity of our presentation to ourselves at the very moment of its impossibility, at the moment of not-being-able-to-be-there?

What does the proper name of an individual signify, suppose it is the proper name 'Jacques Derrida' who appears to us now, perhaps more so now than ever before as *this* absolutely singular and irreplaceable individual? How a proper name, or proper name as such, each proper name in its respective singularity, becomes for us—for the one who has survived—tied to death, to the event of a departure so that with the evocation of this proper name becomes for us immediately a signature of an absence, of a departure without return, that *affects* us—and Levinas (Levinas 2000) says this over and over again so beautifully—with an *affection* which is that of mourning. Is not mourning—and this will perhaps be Levinas' question—more primordial and originary than, let us say, the anxiety for one's 'being-towards-death'? Anxiety would, then, only be secondary to the more originary mourning, and not vice versa.

But this is not what I ask myself today. What intrigues me rather, always, and I could never stop myself wondering, is this: how a proper name is tied to death, *each* proper name *singularly*, with an absence which appears absolutely *singular* and heterogeneous, so that the proper name itself becomes a site, not so much of a self-presence, but the presence of an absence, a signature of the invisible, an apparition of the unapparent that haunts us and that refuses to be interiorised in 'my' self, that remains something un-incorporable and heterogeneous, something strange almost to the point of uncanny and yet familiar, something that dwells within us and yet without us? It is what Derrida thinks with the name, as we know, *specter*,[4] a strange name, in which is evoked something like an excess, an infinite surplus of the name itself—with its excess of mourning, un-incorporable, a kind of remainder—that does not allow itself to be thought within a certain onto-theology that has served as foundation of a philosophical ethics of the West.

Specter: does it not haunt with so much of its mourning in the very name, in the very proper name to which each of us is tied? When parents give us, to each of us singularly, to 'me' *this* proper name, do not they also bestow upon 'me' this gift that is born out of death but that signifies life, 'this' life so that the world will miss this singular existence with/after 'my' death whenever this proper name is evoked, as if this proper name itself has become *spectral*, an invisible-visibility, an absent-presence, a non-proper proper name? I am not sure Derrida asks this question in this way, but I am asking this question, let me say, in the spirit of Derrida: the spectral 'character' (which is not to be taken as an attribute of a Substance) of the proper name and the irreducible mourning that haunts not only whenever 'I' pronounce my 'own' name in solitude or in being-with-others, but more particularly when 'I' pronounce the other's name, the other who has departed without return. What, however, Derrida asks us to think, in so many different ways, is this strange (non) phenomenon like a *specter* that inhabits, or rather ex-habits in any presentation of oneself to oneself, in any presentation of oneself to the other, or the other's presentation to 'me' so that 'one' is tied to the other as if tied to her death—in a relation without relation, in a tie without tie—so that each self-presence, each proper name, is haunted by a non-presence and a non-proper, by an un-incorporable excess, by an infinite surplus, by a non-power, by the outside of what Derrida calls an 'originary melancholy', not for a lost presence but an already effaced presence. What Derrida calls this strange phenomenon in so many names, all singular names—*trace, difference, specter, writing*: to name a few—are the figures, rather dis-figures of that originary mourning. Is not this the very site of a *responsibility*, the condition of the possibility of a responsibility which does not allow itself to be thought within the foundation of a philosophical ethics, a responsibility which is like the *generosity* of the singular, *the generosity of an offering*? If that is so, then this notion of responsibility can only be thought as a gift that is haunted by a mourning insofar as this gift is not exhausted in any circular re-appropriation of the debtor and creditor, in any economic equivalences of values, in any ontological leveling of self to self, self to the other, other to self, or in any temporal figure of the circle, which is the figure of time as circle, the circle as time. One is here reminded of Heidegger's deconstruction in *Being and Time* (1962) of what Heidegger calls 'vulgar' concept of time, which Derrida takes into account, in a very Heideggerian manner, and yet departing from it; it is the deconstruction of the dominant metaphysical determination of time as circular return, where the existential *ecstases* of temporality is reduced, leveled off to the categorical 'nows' in their eternal succession, in the equivalences of each one with the others insofar they belong to the Universal Now.

Thus in Heidegger's *Being and Time* this vulgar concept of time, from which the inauthenticity of gossip, or rumour of *das Man* is indissociable, is guided by the economic reason from which the thought of the gift, the *es gibt* in *Da* of *Da-sein* is to be distinguished. Thus the thought of the gift, *es gibt* of Dasein, which is neither the gift of one entity among the entities 'presently given'

(*Vorhandenheit*), nor 'entities ready to be used' (*Zuhandenheit*), this gift arrives only at that moment of the opening of the circle of equivalences of nows, of the exchange values of nows to the *existential 'da', the-there*, which is not a topological site within the economy of reason, but the moment of a structural opening.

It is the transcendence of the futurity that opens itself in the *giving* of the gift. Therefore the thought of the gift in Heidegger is always the thought of the future and transcendence, and above all, it is the thought of a dying which is neither *perishing* of 'presently given entities' (*Vorhandenheit*), nor *demise*, but a *dying* which the existential analytic alone can have access.[5] One is here reminded of Bataille when he speaks of the 'vulgar' notion of meaning, insofar as this meaning is always a meaning of a death, an invested death, a death that is not without profit, a death that is used up and exchanged within a 'restricted economy'.

What, then, Derrida asks us to think is the demand of a responsibility that is impossible, that does not allow itself to be thought within the economy of a philosophical ethics, within the philosophical ethics of an economy, which is always an economy of values and of time, an economy of death and mourning, an economy of the debtor and creditor, an economy of self and other, the economy of an ontology and a thanatology, an *econo-onto-thanatology*, if I can coin such a strange term. Whether it is in his *Given Time* (1992), or in his *The Gift of Death* (1995), Derrida exposes tirelessly the economic foundation of a philosophical ethics where an economic ethics of responsibility is tied to this *econo-onto-thanatology*, where this responsibility is also a presentation of a certain figure of death, and a certain figure of time, the geometric figure of the circle. The figure of the circle is time as economy; it is the economic figure of time where infinite gift and infinite responsibility itself is annulled when the gift is sought to be inscribed within an equivalences of values. It is this that makes responsibility relate to the impossible, and to mourning, for mourning is *an-economic*, not the mourning that works but the worklessness of a mourning that is irreducible to the process of interiorisation and subjectification, insofar as this process of interiorisation—at least in psychoanalytic thinking of mourning—always appears as the circular return within an economy of conservation of what is negated, of the process of a loss and dissolution, something like what Hegel calls *Aufhebung*. Thus in his *Given Time* Derrida relates the thought of the gift to mourning, if mourning, like the gift, amounts to not-keeping, not-being-able-to keep, as if the affirmation of the gift demands an affirmation which is impossible, the affirmation of forgetting, an affirmative forgetting, which is more originary than a topological displacement, or repression within the economy of memory (dialectical-speculative, or otherwise).

To take the side of death is, thus, never so easy and never so obvious a thing. It is to open to that originary mournfulness in which the gift arrives. This gift is none but the gift of the proper name. A strange gift it is, this proper name, coming from others, from another origin when 'I' am not there, where *there* already occurs an anticipation, an awaiting of a departure so that the proper name becomes for us—and not only for others after our departure—something strange to ourselves; it is the strangeness of our impossibility of an absolute self-identification, the difficulty of self-recognition without a melancholic touch, by virtue of, and precisely in the marks of the very proper name which is supposedly to be singularly 'mine', 'his' or 'her'. In that 'jubilant assumption' of what Jacques Lacan calls 'mis-recognition', there is also a kind of melancholy, an un-assumable melancholy in not-being-able-to assume one's origin and one's death, not-being-able-to make it very 'proper' to oneself. Derrida tirelessly keeps coming back again and again, in the manner of Levinas, to this un-assumable death whenever he comes to speak of Heidegger, in order to think of a responsibility not on the basis of an assumable death, but relating to a death which is an impossible passage. In this sense Derrida is very close to Schelling whom he hardly quotes or refers. In that great book *Philosophical Inquiries into the Nature of Human Freedom* (1936), Schelling thus discovers the origin of freedom and responsibility not on the basis of an assumable death, not on the basis of a condition that can be posited and grounded, not on the basis of a condition that can be made 'proper', one's very 'proper', one's very own. Hence there lies that 'irreducible remainder' of the unconditioned, the inappropriable that cannot be grounded in reason or being; hence there arises, because of this originary finitude, that unappeasable 'veil of sadness' (Schelling 1936: 79) that haunts, like a specter, like a ghost, our finite existence. The possibility of this sadness, so says Schelling, is there even in God insofar as God also has to *come into his existence*. This originary *non-self-co-incidence*, this tearing *apart* of being as a condition of *coming* and *arrival* is not a negation of responsibility, but precisely is the condition of the possibility of responsibility, which occurs as—and what Derrida sometimes calls—the 'gift'; sometimes 'debt', and what Schelling calls 'loan'. Schelling's idea of the 'loan' is not to be thought within the *econo-ontology* of a philosophical ethics, but precisely as *non-economic bestowal*, or originary *donation*, whose *arrival* is from a site wholly otherwise, a destination wholly otherwise insofar as this *loan* has not come from anyone (from an already constituted subject to an already constituted object; from a creditor to a debtor); it is the originary loan that cannot be leveled or homogenized, since this loan does not have any equivalences in finite life; since this loan does not return in a circular re-appropriation to its self-same source. Therefore finitude, instead of a negation of responsibility, precisely makes responsibility possible by placing this gift: this *loan* is outside the circular re-appropriation of the same; it is outside the economy of being-beside-oneself; it is outside the economy (here Schelling is arguing against Hegelian logic of *Aufhebung*) of the ontological leveling of the relation between (unconditional) condition and conditioned. Therefore melancholy for Schelling is no objection; it is the very originary opening to the redemptive joyousness of creative freedom. Schelling calls this joy as *love*.

In his *Given Time* Derrida speaks of the necessity and the demand of the non-recognition of the gift *as* gift as the necessary condition of the gift. For the gift to be gift, the gift must *not* appear as gift; it must not *present* itself as gift; it must not have its time as presence (it must not present itself as gift), as if the gift to be gift, there must not be there anything like the gift. What is it that makes the gift tied to the impossible if not its *event* character, for the event—which is aleatory, irruptive, emerging at an instance of surprise—escapes the logic of the possible. Let me read these beautiful lines from *Given Time*:

> There must be event—and therefore appeal to narrative and event of narrative—for there to be gift, and therefore must be gift or *phenomenon of gift*—for there to be narrative and history. And this event, event of condition and condition of event, must remain in a certain way unforeseeable. The gift, like the event, as event, must *remain* unforeseeable, but remain so without keeping itself. It must let itself be structured by the aleatory . . . That is why the condition common to the gift and the event is a certain unconditionality. (Derrida 1992: 122–23)

A strange logic of the gift: in order for there to be the gift, the gift must not appear within the phenomenological horizon of *the possible, even if it is the 'possibility of impossibilities'.* Thus Derrida's aporetic question: is my death possible?, is at once the question: is the gift possible?, insofar as the gift, like the melancholy of the image that Derrida speaks of when he speaks of the works of Luis Marin, is tied to death, like the melancholy of the proper name that bestowing upon us a name, a signature, a mark, *always already* makes us stranger to ourselves, even before identification, subjectification, self-recognition. The gift does not belong to the logic of property and propriety but to that play of differ*a*nce, which is differ*a*nce as play, differ*a*nce as the impossible.

What is it to take the side of death?

What it is to take the side of death? As if the philosopher 'Jacques Derrida' has already anticipated, awaited his own death at the 'limit of truth', who now towards the end of his life, meditates on death—like Socrates—as if the figure of death here imperceptibly, almost invisibly, secretly has tended towards this figure of the philosopher with a proper name. Is it not the name of name—proper name—in a certain sense, already traversed by death's patience, already traversed by mourning, and by a secret which is death's secret, and death's gift? If the proper name always arises out of the lack of a name, would not what we call 'proper name' be of the prosthetic origin, and therefore not 'proper'?

What is it that ties the proper name to death, and what is it that ties death to gift and to secret, not just in an accidental manner but essentially, in the innermost way such that it concerns the very 'proper' of the proper name, that makes the proper name at once strange and familiar, proper and non-proper, visible and yet invisible, in another word, *spectral*?

It appears as if, to our first glance, that there is an absence of an ethics here, a disavowal of responsibility, and a refusal to assume decision in the face of one's death, in the face of others' death. Can there be an ethics of mourning, a responsibility in mourning, in so far as it appears already here of an impossibility to assume responsibility, to allow 'death's decision'—to use Kierkegaard's phrase—to be borne out of responsibility's earnestness, which is the earnestness concerning opening of self to self, and self to the other(s), this absolutely singular earnestness of existence concerning—what Heidegger says—being's 'being-towards- death'? How can one be resolute in the face of death, how can one be decisive and be responsible if death does not allow gathering of self to self unto its very interior ground, if death has not acquired the solidity of the underground earth with its subterranean passages, with its secrets and the smell of the moist soil?

What is it to take the side of death? For it seems obvious to us what is it to take the side of 'life'. Would it not be to give oneself training to learn, as Montaigne says, 'to philosophize is to learn how to die' (Montaigne 2003: 67–81), to give oneself death, to give oneself the gift of death so that each one dies—as Heidegger says—one's own death? If that is so, the figure of death is tied up with the very figure of the philosopher, with the proper name of the philosopher 'Socrates', or 'Jacques Derrida' or 'Martin Heidegger', with the very proper-ness of this *proper* name, with the name of this proper *name.* And above all it is mourning, mourning that is learnt and has become 'work'—of interiorisation and subjectification process—and the other mourning in its worklessness, infinite mourning, and excessive mourning, without any inscription and without any monuments, without archives and without works, without history and without concept. It will perhaps be interesting and fascinating to undertake the whole history of philosophy as the history of thinking, ruminating, meditating on the figures of death, the figures of their own death and the death of others, which is also to be the history of the experiences of mourning, mourning that affects, traces, wounds, tears thinking, philosophical thinking, not excluding even those who like Spinoza, Montaigne, Cixous and more, take the side of life. It will be interesting and fascinating to undertake a history of the experiences of responsibility and ethics as the history of this experience of mourning where the very notions of 'responsibility' and 'ethics' themselves are under question, each time, as eruption of each singular experience of mourning, each time anew, each time the beginning and the end of the world. It should be able to bring out the secret that ties philosophy itself, not merely the philosopher to death, but to philosophy's death, philosophy's incessant mourning of *its* death, as if philosophy *always already* has to present to itself, by a necessary logic, its own absence and departure, its exits and its abandonment. The history of philosophy would, then, be the history as abandonment, or better, the history of the experiences of abandonment. Thus when Heidegger speaks of the *event of appropriation* (*Ereignis*), which is strangely, the event of dispropriation; or when Hölderlin sings of the fugitive Gods, and withdrawal of the 'heavenly fire', is it not, in each instance, the abandonment that is at stake; abandonment that is tied up with the destiny of a thinking, which is also thinking of ethics, of ethics as destiny?

The death of Socrates

In a proposition in his *Ethics* Spinoza claims: 'A free man thinks nothing less than of death; and his wisdom is a meditation not of death, but of life' (Spinoza 1955: 232). We know is this wise man whose meditation is not of death but of life. It is none but the very figure of the philosopher. There is Socrates who, of all philosophers, is the very figure of 'philosopher', not in the sense that he is greater philosopher than others, but because his thinking in its purity, as Heidegger argues, did not need the draft of the written, and who says to Phaedo before drinking Hemlock these words: 'Those who apply themselves to philosophy in the proper way are doing no more nor less than to prepare themselves for the moment of dying and the state of death' (Plato 1972: 103).

This moment of Socrates' dying is not one moment among moments of the history of philosophical thinking; it is the very moment of the birth of 'philosophy', the moment when philosophy became for the first time self-conscious of its being as 'philosophy', the moment of philosophy's opening itself to itself, the *event* of philosophy's *coming to presence* to itself, the *event* of philosophy's eruption into its own presence, as if at that very moment an abyss has opened up at the very heart of philosophy's beginning, that is of death and a mourning that has henceforth haunted, like a specter, the whole history of philosophy against which Montaigne asserts his refusal to be sad, and Spinoza refuses to meditate on death. At the very birth of philosophy's becoming there was a trembling and a cry, a seizure and an absence that has already opened up philosophy at that very moment of its coming to its abyss, and also, at that very moment of seizure there is felt—and Hegel[6] dramatizes this moment when he speaks of looking death in its face—the necessity to look death in its face, to tarry with it, and to discover at the very moment of its dismembering its truth (to salvage from the shipwreck of truth) the possibility of a decision and responsibility, of an ethics and an aesthetics of dying, and hence, there has to emerge, at that very moment, the necessity of a training—not just learning to die and to prepare oneself for the moment of dying—but a training to sacrifice oneself, and on the basis of this tragic-heroic pathos of the sacrificial to be able to constitute an ethics of responsibility and of decision. The moment of dismemberment also has to be—and this is the strange paradox—the moment of gathering, coinciding of self to self, self to the world, of self to the others and to the divine, as if, as in the classic interpretation of tragic drama, the atonement is here not so much of guilt, but of mourning, so that there be *work*, there be work *at* mourning for the sake of an ethics, of decision, of responsibility. The moment of the birth of philosophy, which has felt in its veins the seizure of death, is also the moment of the birth of an ethics of responsibility and of decision, which has henceforth decided in advance the whole destinal thinking of responsibility and of ethics *as such*. Therefore this ethics of responsibility is born with the confrontation with death, founded upon death, upon this impossibility or 'non-actuality' called 'death'; this ethics is born in this encounter with a gaze of an abyss which now, when being domesticated, speaks the language of responsibility and decision, of sacrifice for the other's death, and for the sake of truth. The language of this ethics is this language of conversions, which also means preservation, elevation and negation, of nothing less than death than which, of all name is the name of the impossible.

There, then, occurs as the very condition of a philosophical ethics a figure of death as an economic figure. One pays death, one gives oneself one's death for greater gain, which is for Socrates 'immortality'. The figure of the philosopher is the site of a sacrifice. This is the only consolation for the figure of the philosopher through which the figure of death speaks, that philosopher is nothing but this demonic, monstrous site—neither completely divine nor completely human—where truth occurs in its earnestness, and this truth takes away from death—to evoke Rosenzweig—its 'poisonous sting', its 'pestilential breath' (Rosenzweig 2005: 9). To be a philosopher, and to philosophize is to train oneself for this truth, to care for one's own death for the sake of a care for truth, which is to open up the heart of existence of the philosopher, to open up this heart towards the abyss, and in this opening allowing truth to pass as truth, to welcome truth as the event of an arrival. Then there would be melancholy no more, for with that event a future is opened up, and death is mastered, at least domesticated, if death means nothing less and no more than the end of time and the end of future. It is in this anticipation of the futurity that has opened up from the very heart of death, from the very abyss of a dissolution, that Socrates asks the foolish women of Athens who are not wise because they have not yet learnt how to die, to go away when the philosopher dies, and in this anticipation of a futurity that Hegel's asks the naive consciousness not to lament vain death, death that does not have future, death that could not be *work*, like 'swallowing the mouthful of water', useless death, vain death, imposture of death.[7] The joy of life therefore—Hegel would perhaps have responded in this way to Spinoza—cannot shrink from the thought of death, but to be joyous means to rescue a self from death, a life from death, *converting* death into life, another life, a *resurrected* life. Therefore there is life and life's joyousness—if it has to be authentic, proper, and not merely immediate, vain sensuousness—only as *uplifted* (*Aufheben*) joy, a *resurrected* life, not life that is immediately given, but becoming *otherwise* than anything that is given as this life, another language of life, and another meaning of joy. What is the meaning of 'ethical' and 'ethics' if not this *becoming* different, this *becoming* other of oneself, to be able to give oneself another life and another death, and becoming responsible for this decisive becoming of becoming other? Does not Kierkegaard too says of ethics something of this sort in *Concluding Unscientific Postscript*, and does not Rosenzweig (2005) speak of it when he discusses Gilgamesh's confrontation with death?: that ethics is nothing less than this passing, traversing, confronting death as death; or better, ethics for this singular individual, or perhaps even for a community takes birth when it confronts death as death, when it feels at the very heart of existence, in its bones and marrow, in its veins the seizure and trembling of death. As if this truth, this event of ethics and decision, of responsibility and freedom is the very *gift* of death, which is not this or that gift, but the very gift-ness of the gift. The ethics of an individual self, and also a community is born precisely at that moment when, in its confrontation with death, the self feels the necessity to *become* otherwise than its mere immediate existence, and when this necessity demands simultaneously a series of training, or a series of practices, discursive or otherwise, and an ethical discourse on what is called, 'care for death'.

Let me come back to Derrida now after this long detour. When Derrida takes the side of death, is he speaking of ethics and responsibility with the same gesture, in relation to death, and above all, of gift as an infinite relation to the other who is yet to come; of a futurity in its messianic intensity; of a futurity whose thought is no stranger to the thought of death but that opens up from very heart of an abyss, which is death's abyss? To take the side of death is to take the side of responsibility and of ethics; it is to be indebted, in mourning, for the gift given to 'me' even before this 'I' have asked for, given in a time immemorial and ancient, in a time before time. Therefore the thought of gift and responsibility always accompanies mourning, and is tied to the thought of death. Yet is this death that Derrida takes the side of the same figure of death that has haunted the very figure of the philosopher from Plato to Heidegger, death that in its very impossibility and abyss gifts the philosopher a self, the possibility of gathering unto itself, and also the possibility through death of becoming other than oneself, as an ethical self in its decisive sense, which assumes responsibility and decision at the very moment of dismemberment? If, as Heidegger says, decisions are always taken at the limit, that means, out of the undecidable, then in all decisive decisions a madness, even death watches over. Is this death that Derrida has taken the side of when he speaks of responsibility and of the gift, this gift of death to oneself, to give oneself death? Or is there another figure or disfigure of death, and other thoughts of responsibility and gift? It is this question that I now turn.

Taking recourse to Patôcka

In his very beautiful book called *The Gift of Death*, reading Jan Patocˇka and Søren Kierkegaard, Derrida brings out Patočka's history of the emergence of an ethics of responsibility as a discontinuous, disruptive history of various experiences of confrontation with death's seizure and with this confrontation arising of an ethics of care for death, to give oneself the gift of death, so that in this gathering of self to self, in this whole process of subjectification and interiorization, there is felt the necessity of decision and ethical responsibility to acknowledge the historicity, this historicity of discontinuity itself, which is for Patočka the history of Christian-European responsibility. This history that Patočka recounts, which is history of responsibility and history of an ethics of decision has known two events of rupture or discontinuity: the event of philosophy's birth—which is here the event of Socrates' death and Plato's writing—and the event of Christianity. Thus the history of the thought of responsibility, the historicity which the historical man refuses to admit, passes through these two events of mutation: the event of Platonic philosophy's conversion, subjugation, interiorization of the orgiastic mystery, and the event of Christianity's repression, conversion, and interiorization of the Platonic mystery. With each mutation there occurs a new structure of responsibility, and with each new structure of responsibility there is a new confrontation with death: in the case of Platonic philosophy it is the responsibility that arises with the care for death, *meletē Thanatos* that demands subjugation of the orgiastic and demonic mystery, and with the event of Christianity it is the *mysterium tremendum*, the fear and trembling in the experience of the sacrificial gift, in the face of the absolute being wholly other whose gaze transfixes us, and commands us to be responsible, whose gaze, the gaze that looks at us, we cannot see. In both the events there occurs a simultaneous mutation and the *coming to presence* of a new responsibility which is born out of death as death's gift, and each time with this simultaneous process of mutation and coming to presence there occurs a new structure of responsibility, a new secret and the sacred that follows, however, the same logic of movement as the one before, which is the logic of conversion and interiorization: that of preserving within oneself what is negated and through this very preservation-negation to uplift itself, very much like Hegelian logic of *Aufhebung,* or what Freud understands as the *work of mourning*. In this way, so Derrida points out, the logic of the historicity of the history which Patočka recounts is the logic of a certain economy of the experience of death and a certain economy of mourning as the process of an interiorization and subjectification that serves as the very foundational condition of the possibility of an ethics and a politics of responsibility, which is understood as this *being-able-to-be-beside-oneself* in setting apart from oneself, like Heidegger's—despite Heidegger's existential critique of the Christocentric onto-theology—like Heidegger's *Sorge*, care for this 'being-towards-death', care for this 'possibility of all impossibilities' so that 'my' death be 'my' death, very authentic, *eigntlich*, which defines the very proper-ness of the proper. The notion of the gift and responsibility is thus inscribed in the economy of a sacrificial death and in this economy of mourning—that of interiorization and subjectification—where the gift of death is always the gift of 'my' death, this being able to give and receive one's own death. Thus the secret of responsibility that arises out of this historicity is to be distinguished from the orgiastic, demonic secret, which amounts to be saying that responsibility emerges at that moment when there occurs subordination, or conversion or repression of the orgiastic, demonic secrets. Yet, since repression never eliminates what it represses, the orgiastic and the demonic threatens to come back as sacred enthusiasm, in a kind of haunting, spectral return: for example, the French Revolution. Patočka thus warns us against this spectral presence of the orgiastic whose return finds expression in various forms of totalitarianism that Europe has seen, and hence his thesis: complete subordination, conversion of the orgiastic under a responsibility which is *mysterium tremendum*, which is for Patočka, in his own heretical way, a Christian-European responsibility. What Derrida sees in this notion of responsibility that arises in its confrontation with *mysterium tremendum* is a certain politics of death, which is Patočka's Christian politics, a politics that is inseparable from the certain experience of the sacrificial gift and secret.

Yet what is fascinating and interesting about Patočka's heretical history of the notion of responsibility, which is also history of secret, is Patočka's heretical deconstruction of the philosophical ethics that is based upon a certain economic reason: knowledge. Responsibility for Patočka is always thus taken at the limit of the calculable and programmable, each time singular, and each time anew, for each time one must assume the arriving of the event of that trembling which is imminent and yet incalculable, the undecidable seizure, irreducible to anything like truth or cognition. In other words, the demand of decision and responsibility, in its absolute singularity and irreducibility, does not completely belong to the realm of generality where there occurs the equivalences of values, where there is, as in a civilization completely under the sway of the technological, the leveling of singularity to the form of boredom, which is not anything neutral, but the very avatar of the return of the orgiastic and demonic.

Responsibility beyond the realm of generality, which is the confrontation with the *mysterium tremendum*, is for Kierkegaard the paradox of the *instant* (*Augenblick*), which escapes the circularity of time; the economic figure of time as circle, and which appears for mortals as that which Kierkegaard calls, *death's decision*. The paradox of the instant of responsibility which is death's decision, for Kierkegaard, is the very paradox of responsibility. Derrida here brings out, in his usual brilliant manner, this paradox in the following manner: that absolute responsibility, responsibility to the absolutely singular other, the wholly other, the other who cannot be thought within the economy of the generality that defines the realm of the ethical, is also, paradoxically, an irresponsibility without justification, seeing from the point of view of the ethical. As if an absolute responsibility demands, accompanies an unforgivable, unjustifiable, unethical irresponsibility, as in the case of Abraham's sacrificing his son. Through this story, or fable, Kierkegaard's de Silentio (1983) brings out, not so much the justification of the irresponsibility and invalidity of the claim of the ethical—in fact Kierkegaard's de Silentio repeatedly comes to accentuate the unforgivable character of that horrifying irresponsibility, and thus pushing the unforgivable character of that irresponsibility to the limit—but the irreducible heterogeneity between the *an-economic* of a responsibility to the absolutely singular (to the wholly other), and an *economy* of the sacrificial death that is based upon the logic of creditor and debtor: the economy of the re-appropriation through gift, which is the gift of death that is inscribed in the econo-geometric figure of time as circle. The instant of death, the instant which the narrator in Maurice Blanchot's beautiful short story *The Instant of My Death* (2000) evokes, is the instant that escapes the circularity of time that re-appropriates the gift. This *an-economic* instant therefore cannot be inscribed within the equivalences of values, within the system of generality. This instant is the figure of death, or rather is the dis-figuring of death, for here is the confrontation with the *mysterium tremendum* that seizes hold of us and cannot be communicated in ethical signification, but that can only be said in the manner of what Kierkegaard calls 'indirect communication'. Hence, the secret is tied to responsibility, which is here always the question of language; language that cannot be reduced to the logic of manifestation, like Hegelian logic of a phenomenology, but the *event of language* itself as gift. The gift of death has a different secret than the secret of an economy of return to the same, than the homogenizing of the relation between a creditor and the debtor. The gift, then, in the instant of its arrival, is indissociable from the instant of death. It is the structural moment of an opening of the figure of the circle. As such it does not have the figure itself in any presentation of itself as such. *This figure of death does not have its own figure.* This figure of death which does not have its own figure is what I call, following Kierkegaard, 'secret', which, as death's secret, is also the secret of language. It is here, in this relation to secret, that a thought of responsibility, at the limit of a philosophical foundation of ethics, is to be developed: an impossible thought of responsibility, for it is tied to the impossible itself, to a death without profit and without investment.

La mort et l'amour

What is it, then, for Derrida to take the side of death? Does it mean negation of anything like what manifests to us as 'life', the joyousness of life, its exuberance and plenitude, its innocence and warmth? Or, does it mean the disavowal of responsibility, for does not responsibility mean always, first and foremost, responsibility for the one who is alive and living, so that one says 'let the dead bury the dead'? Does the one who takes the side of death know what he takes the side of, in so far as death is not one phenomenon among others but a presentation that never presents itself as presence, like the very non-appearing appearance of the specter, of the gift and of the secret? Perhaps death does not have its own time, and yet, in some obscure way, we mortals who live, feel this intimate, profound, connection of death with time, the relation that cannot be said in a language of signification(that is, in the language of what Kierkegaard, referring to Hegel, calls the language of 'generality').

There is a scene in the movie on Derrida by Kirby Dick: Derrida, in responding to a question on love, *l'amour*, and as if pretending not to have heard correctly, asks: are you asking of death?, thus playing with the word *la mort*, which means in French 'death'. Derrida, then, goes on to talk of Narcissus, which is at once a love story and a story of death. To give oneself love alone—

which is Narcissistic love—is to give oneself death: in both cases it is blindness. Therefore Narcissus weeps, not because he does not see at all, but because he sees only himself and none other, for to see oneself alone and not to see others, is blindness. He does not see the gift of the other, of the other's love and the other's death. This blindness is not the blindness arising of excessive light, or excessive seeing, but the blindness of an economic reason, of an economic love and an economy of death, which precisely in its blindness exceeds that economic reason. It is the blindness not being able to see the gift.

Taking the side of Derrida

What is it to take the side of death? Each of us takes the side of something or other: of death or of life; but the strange thing is that this taking sides is never intentional, self-conscious, or made with deliberation on the basis of knowledge but rather, it is as if we are always already taken side of when we think that it is 'we' who take our side. To take the side of Death, like Derrida, is to know in a strange kind of knowledge that we do not yet read what we write, what death writes in us, through us, beyond us, and when we think that we can read death's writing, death has already read us, long back, when we were not there, when we will no longer be there.

NOTES

1. If the relation to the other is essentially that of a (non) relation to the other's finitude, then this (non)relation is already always that of 'affection': an inconsolable mourning, 'an excess in death'. Thus Levinas speaks of 'grief' with the disappearance of the other who would not return. Affection in mourning the dying of the other without return affects us inconsolably beyond knowledge, certitude and excess of every consolation. Levinas thus says, 'as if there were an excess in death. It is a simple passage, a simple departure and yet a source of emotion contrary to every effort at consolation'

(Levinas 2000: 9). In this sense there is a close proximity, not without distance, with Derrida's notion of 'preoriginary mourning'. Derrida, however, speaks of this 'pre-originary' mourning in relation to the question of the 'origin' which is always already 'absent' (if one can speak of it as 'absent') and therefore that cannot be thought within any metaphysics of self-presence. However for Derrida, the other is not merely the other person. What, to me, Derrida seems to be deconstructing is, not so much an absence of mourning in Levinas' thought, but mourning for the other who is only 'person', the other man. It is in this context Derrida raises the question of the animal. This article, following Derrida as well Levinas, attempts to think our (non)relation to death in a more originary than Heideggerian 'Being-towards-death' and anxiety as its fundamental *Grundstimmung*. Thus mourning is thought here, not as form of mourning, but a more originary attunement than anxiety in its 'Being-towards-death'.

2. For the question of the prosthesis of origin, see Derrida's *Monolingualism of the Other, or Prosthesis of Origin* (1998). *Eigentlich* is one of the concepts that Martin Heidegger uses in *Being and Time* (1962).
3. For Derrida's discussion on the question of the name see *On the Name* (1995a).
4. For Derrida's elaboration of the notion of 'specter' see *Specters of Marx* (1994).
5. I refer to Derrida's *Aporias* (1993) for Derrida's deconstruction of Heideggerian distinctions among *perishing, demise* and *dying*.
6. 'Death, if that is what we want to call this non-actuality, is of all things the most dreadful, and to hold fast what is dead requires the greatest strength . . . But the life of Spirit is not the life that shrinks from death and keeps itself untouched by devastation, but rather the life that endures it and maintains itself in it . . . Spirit is this power only by looking the negative in the face, and tarrying with it' (Hegel 1998: 19).
7. Thus in his *Lectures on the Philosophy of Religion*, Hegel writes, 'The natural, simple self-emancipation of the finite from its finiteness is death. This is the renunciation of the finite, and here what the

natural life is itself implicitly is made explicit really and actually. The sensuous life of what is individual or particular has its end in death. Particular experiences or sensations as particular are transient; one supplants the other, one impulse or other drives away the another . . . In death the finite is shown to be annulled and absorbed. But death is only abstract negation of what is implicitly negative; it is itself a nullity, it is revealed a nullity. But explicit nullity is at the same time nullity which has been done away with, and is the return to the positive. Here cessation, liberated from finiteness, comes in. Death does not present itself to consciousness as this emancipation from finiteness, but this higher view of death is found in thought, and indeed even in popular conceptions, in so far as thought is active in them' (Hegel 1962: 182).

REFERENCES

Blanchot, Maurice, *The Writing of the Disaster*, trans. Ann Smock (Lincoln: University of Nebraska Press, 1995).

Blanchot, Maurice and Jacques Derrida, *The Instant of My Death/ Demure: Fiction and Testimony*, trans. Elizabeth Rottenberg (Stanford, CA: Stanford University Press, 2000).

Derrida, Jacques, *Given Time I. Counterfeit Money*, trans. Peggy Kamuf (Chicago: Chicago University Press, 1992).

Derrida, Jacques, *Aporias*, trans. Thomas Dutoit (Stanford, CA: Stanford University Press, 1993).

Derrida, Jacques, *Specters of Marx: The State of the Debt, The Work of Mourning and The New International*, trans. Peggy Kamuf (London: Routledge, 1994).

Derrida, Jacques, *The Gift of Death*, trans. David Wills (Chicago: Chicago University Press, 1995).

Derrida, Jacques, *On the Name*, ed. Thomas Dutoit, trans. David Wood, John P. Leavey and Ian McLeod (Stanford, CA: Stanford University Press, 1995a).

Derrida, Jacques, *Monolingualism of the Other or Prosthesis of Origin*, trans. Patrick Mensah (Stanford, CA: Stanford University Press, 1998).

Derrida, Jacques, *H. C. for Life, That Is to Say . . .*, trans. Laurent Milesi and Stefan Herbrechter (Stanford, CA: Stanford University Press, 2006).

Hegel, G.W.F., *Lectures on the Philosophy of Religion*, Vol. 1, trans. E.B. Speirs (London: Routledge and Kegan Paul, 1962).

Hegel, G.W.F., *Phenomenology of Spirit*, trans. A.V. Miller (Delhi: Motilal Benarasidass, 1998).

Heidegger, Martin, *Being and Time*, trans. John Macquarrie and Edward Robinson (New York: Harper and Row, 1962).

Kant, Immanuel, 'The Groundwork of the Metaphysics of Morals', in *Kant's Practical Philosophy*, trans. Mary J. Gregory (Cambridge: Cambridge University Press, 1996), pp. 37-108.

Kierkegaard, Søren, *Fear and Trembling* and *Repetition*, trans. Howard Hong and Edna H. Hong (Princeton: Princeton University Press, 1983).

Levinas, Emmanuel, *God, Death and Time*, trans. Bettino Bergo (Stanford, CA: Stanford University Press, 2000).

Montaigne, Michel de, 'That to Philosophize is to Learn to Die', in *The Complete Works*, trans. Donald M. Frame (London: Everyman's Library, 2003), pp. 67–81.

Plato, 'Phaedo', in *The Trail and Execution of Socrates*, trans. Peter George (London: The Folio Society, 1972).

Rosenzweig, Franz, *The Star of Redemption*, trans. Barbara E. Galli (Wisconsin: The University of Wisconsin Press, 2005).

Schelling, F.W.J. von, *Philosophical Inquiries into the Nature of Human Freedom*, trans. James Gutmann (La Salle, IL: Illinois, 1936).

Spinoza, *On the Improvement of the Understanding, The Ethics, Correspondence*, trans. R.H.M. Elwes (New York: Dover, 1955).

Derrida's tympan: mourning, philosophy, literature

This paper attempts to think again, in the spirit of Jacques Derrida and with his help, the relationship between philosophy and literature. Taking the questions of death and mourning as its central concerns, I attempt to think literature as pointing to the space of the outside that is beyond the closure of philosophy. Literature, then, is the space of excess—of mourning and of the worklessness of dying—which cannot be enclosed within the economy of the metaphysics of presence. At stake here that of is renewing of the very ethico-political question of our existence that demands that our ethical responsibility be opened up, beyond any metaphysics of presence, to the infinitude of the Other who advents from the extremity of the future, a future that cannot be enclosed within any immanence of a dialectical-speculative thought.

Specters of death

> In Being-there-and-then, the negation is still directly one with the Being and this negation is what we call a Limit (Boundary). A thing is what it is, only in and by reason of its limit. We cannot therefore regard the limit as only external to being which is then and there. It rather goes through and through the whole of such existence. (Hegel 1975: 136).

> The self-knowing Spirit knows not only itself but also the negative of itself or its limit: to know one's limit is to know how to sacrifice oneself. This sacrifice is the externalization in which Spirit displays the process of its becoming Spirit in the form of *free contingent happening*, intuiting itself pure Self as Time outside it, and equally its Being as Space. The last becoming of Spirit, Nature, is its living immediate Becoming; Nature, the externalized Spirit, is in its existence nothing but this eternal externalization of its continuing existence and the movement which reinstitutes the Subject. (Hegel 1998: 492).

It is death that will be contemplated here—the death of philosophy and of literature—death that of all terrible things is the most terrible and yet that must be maintained[1], death which is the limit of all thought and sense: the impossibility of all that is possible, the immeasurable death that is beyond all measures, and that is the measure of all things, death that constitutes the very existentiality of the mortal being as "human", death that is beyond all knowledge and even beyond the Absolute Knowledge, beyond that negativity of the concept, death that works and death that refuses to work for universal history.

It is of death that will be contemplated here, and we shall see that it is rather the question of *limit*. Above all we shall see, thinking with the help of Jacques Derrida, it is not simply the dialectical-speculative limit between two concepts but that of that infinite *limit* between literature and philosophy itself.

The worklessness of mourning

Let us say, to begin with, there is more than one limit, or at least two, and they limit each other. Let us say, there is more than one modality of thinking death—or, at least two—and that they are non-contemporary and non-simultaneous in their (non) relationship with each other: between them an abyss disrupts any continuity and any self-foundation. The abyss here does not function like the self-foundational principle of logical judgment, that of predicative proposition. Rather, it is a dehiscence or a caesura that holds together and yet separates each from the other in their distance and proximity in such a way that such a distance calls for proximity and proximity interminably falls forth its distantiation from itself. This is, however, no mere jest of words. What we are trying to think here, in a certain spirit of Jacques Derrida if not in letter, a certain (non)phenomenon that cannot be thought on the basis of what Derrida calls "metaphysics of presence". This (non)phenomenon—a phenomenon which no phenomenology of eidetic consciousness can ever formalize—is the very event of death which arrives, as if, from a site of the extremity of the future. This event arriving from the extremity of time—which is thus the very limit of the "metaphysics of presence"—is the event of the limit that exceeds the dominant metaphysics of presence. There is always something in excess of the (non)phenomenon of the event—which is here the event of death to which no mastery is applied, and to which no phenomenology of light and presence can attain its cognition.[2]

Here out thought, which is following to a certain extent in the spirit of Jacques Derrida, is also in a certain proximity (and also distant) to the thought of Martin Heidegger. For Heidegger's *Being and Time* too death is the event whose radical futurity first of all opens Dasein to itself. This inextricable finitude of existence for Heidegger is inseparably tied up with the question of truth understood as *Aletheia* where the unconcealment or disclosure, as the readers of Heidegger know, is inseparable from Heidegger's deconstruction of the dominant metaphysical determination of truth as *adaequatio* in that the (non)phenomenon of *Aletheia* is thought to be more originary event of Being than truth determined as *adaequatio*. To illuminate the problem here is an immense task which is neither possible nor necessary here. Yet we must say, *in passim*, that the rift or the abyss that is opened up here cannot be filled with the *Causa Sui* of God's self-presence, or *Parousia* of the Subject: this abyss is the very *spacing* where the possibility for an ethical thought is prepared in Jacques Derrida's works, in distant-proximity to Heidegger's ontological difference between being and Being. It is this abyss that is opened by the death of God. We know it from the mouth of that madman who once came down to the teeming market place with a lantern in his hands, and thus uttered this most terrible of all news: God is dead.

How that is to be thought?: this most terrible thought, the limit-thought that is beyond all measure, namely, the abyss that is opened up by the death of the God. How to name this abyss that is non-proper of all appropriations, the unnamable itself? To name the unnamable is to stutter like Samuel Beckett's character, as if he has lost its tongue which, as the poet Hölderlin poetizes, is lost in the foreign land when the God has departed, and one cannot even trace back its fugitive footprints back to their presence. It is as if the death of God is at once so overwhelming with a mournfulness, and yet so relieving, a mourning that is beyond all consolation, for no new God has arrived yet and there is not yet a celebration of a 'speculative Good Friday' (Hegel 1977: 190-91). A philosophical thinking that seeks to inaugurate itself here in confrontation with this abyss must take into account what is at stake in this event of the death of God. What is at thus at stake in this thought of death is that of the abyss which no metaphysics of the Subject—which is the dominant metaphysics of the West—can assume or master.

It appears as if philosophical thinking has something to do with an excess that arrives with the event of death, that is, what Derrida calls 'originary mourning' which the metaphysics of presence cannot master. It is as if an originary finitude and its unappeasable mourning *always already*, in an immemorial past, open existence to its truth that is to philosophy itself. It is as if this infinite mourning is the very sense—if it can at all be denominated as "sense"—of my responsibility towards the other that disrupts the unity of my knowledge and the sense of the world[3]. In the *always already* of non-self-presence (the immemorial that lies beyond any metaphysics of self-presence), even beyond being's ecstatic opening to itself, this opening is already opened by a tear, by a wound in the very heart of hearts over the other's death. Henceforth, this immemorial opening, which has never begun in time (because it has always already begun) opens "me" to the infinitude of the other to which "I" is responsible, that is, not in my self-presence, and without ever accomplishing *parousia* of my being.

Let me propose here, then, after these initial remarks: that Jacques Derrida's thought is one of mourning and it is always a mourning of thought, thought's mourning for the other who has *always already* escaped thought, or thought's power to think. Thinking mourns, not for its lost presence, but that it mourns of the other's finitude that has never been present in my self-presence: it is this mourning of what is *always already* lost is the limit of all that thinkable; it is the very excess of thought. It exceeds the light of intelligibility of ontology of presence. Here, then, comes another proposition that I hope to think here: that Jacques Derrida's thought is one of limit, or rather the limit of the one, the limit of the 'being-at-the-limit', the limit of 'Being-there-and-then'. It is the question of thinking the limitlessness of the limit that would be other than the speculative-dialectical limit that posits its limit only to incorporate itself within the philosophical closure. It would not have—unlike the Hegelian metaphysics of presence—the dialectical–speculative movement of *Aufhebung*, that is, the form as negativity. It is thus another limit than the dialectical-speculative limit as negativity (which is the limit between two concepts). Between the concept of the limit as negativity and the infinite limit of mourning there is utmost proximity, and yet a distance, something like an abyss that separates them which, following Derrida, we can call "undecidable". It is the question of the limit that we are pursuing here that does not belong to philosophy, which is not immanent to the philosophical discourse of the Subject's *Parousia*. It is rather the question of the limit of the philosophical discourse itself, and what this *limit* exposes itself to, and opens itself towards: to the infinitude of the other, to the measurelessness of the wholly otherwise that arrives from the extremity of time, that is, from the site of pure future.

Yet, is it not that philosophy too assumes the prerogative to think its limit that means, its death—death that is the most terrible limit of all—that founds and grounds nothing other than being? Thus 'the last philosopher of the Book' (as Derrida calls Hegel) also knows that the Book (or, system of Absolute Knowledge which is the totality of all that is knowable) begins with mourning. The origin of the system is an irreducible experience of mourning, an essential self-diremption that rends being asunder. In this way, the Book or system is already exposed to its limit only insofar as the Book itself is the limit here that limits itself only *in sight of* its very realization of itself. If philosophy has assumed in Hegel's writing the name of the Book, then the Book of philosophy assumes its task to think its limit as its *very* limit, its *own* limit. In this sense for Hegel there cannot be infinite limit that cannot be subsumed within the immanence of its self-presence; there can only be limit that can always be its own other, its very other, its own positing other. Such is the prerogative of the Book, its advent and its adventure, its event character which is only a reductive process of its immanent generation: there is no radical extremity of time from the pure event of future erupts in the midst of being and that surprises us in its wholly other phenomenality. The other here is only immanent other, one's own other and which is not outside of the fold of philosophy. Hegel's metaphysical system, therefore, cannot think the radicality of the pure event or the pure eruption of future, the excess of the limit which is otherwise than negativity, the immemorial opening that first of all open us to truth and to the other, before any self-presence of its meaning. If there is at all an opening to the event of death within the dialectical discourse of philosophy, it is employed for the sake of profit—of meaning and knowledge. It appears that philosophy profits from death in an unforeseen manner, in the most unique way, to which Georges Bataille (Bataille 1997: 279-300), more than any other philosopher appeals to our attention:

that by employing death into the service of meaning, philosophy derives from death the very possibility of production of the world. Thus, death must not go in vain without eliciting profit from it: this is how the Hegelian cunning of Reason actualizes its totality. The Book is now closed; for it has now brought under its jurisdiction the world it produced itself, having been able to name everything—including the absence of being, that is, death itself.

It is here that I think Jacques Derrida's thinking takes its point of departure. What we have learnt to call this gesture or style of thinking as "deconstruction" lies in this: that having named everything—supposing the Book says everything—having exhausted all its possibility of meaning and presence, what else would it name if not this very exhaustion itself (since nothing more remained to be named) that, in the infinity of its fatigue, has abandoned the Book, for the infinite negativity of naming would not stop naming? This infinity of naming, if this negativity really would be pushed to its limitless limit, would now overflow or exceed beyond the closure of the Book.

> *It is outside the Book, beyond all immanent form of its closure that deconstruction ceaselessly affirms. Deconstruction here is deconstruction of philosophy itself, at least in its certain form that has become dominant in the West. This is the paradoxical logic of the Book. It must* always already *be allowed to be named, by another mode of dying and another naming that refuses to be named, by another mode of dying and another mourning that in its very abundance, precisely because of its excess misses something, lacks its name and is powerless. This other mourning is excessive, for one always mourns either too much or not yet enough, as if it will drown the world in its tears. Even if one is exhausted by mourning, mourning forever inexhaustible, abandons itself to the space of the outside. This outside is the outside of philosophy itself that never completely belongs to philosophy. It is the very limitless limit of philosophy.*

This mourning without measure at the event of death would not allow itself to be thought within the sense of philosophy's self-presence. Outside all meaning and all naming, the event of death opens time itself beyond its re-insistence of self-presence to the extremity of time, that is, from a future always yet *to* arrive. This philosophical system that assumes the closure of the Book attempts to think this death only by economizing it and by determining it as essentially economical. One here remembers of Plato's absence when Socrates drank his poison. The philosopher absent himself from the scene of death so that the meaning of death may be saved, so that this discourse call "philosophy" may be possible, so that philosophical knowledge may not be drowned in the abyss and the excess of mourning. *It is as if the repression of mourning constitutes the very possibility of philosophy.* It is not for nothing that Plato banished the poets—the tragic poets among them most, for mourning knows no bounds; it is excessive to the very measure and *ratio* of justice. It is therefore only fit for women: this pure expenditure of meaning, this sheer loss of time beyond recuperation and reparation, the sheer wastage of being's possibility and capacity. The ancient quarrel that Plato alludes to in his *Republic* takes its measure from this excess: that is, philosophy's disavowal of mourning, its economic desire to save meaning and knowledge from the sheer expenditure of tears and prayers. And we shall see that here the question of literature itself is at stake: that is, repression of poetry, specially certain kind of poetry that evokes this excessive and measureless mourning.

This excess of philosophy, this limitless limit of philosophy which does not belong to the immanent closure of the philosophical discourse, it is this excess that opens philosophical discourse to the radical alterity of the pure future. Thus it is the question of thinking *differance*, not so much of dialectical difference (which reduces difference to opposition) but an infinite difference between the dialectical modality of thinking death (that constitutes sense and closure for the philosophical discourse) and the other death, the death of the other that opens the Book to the outside from where mourning takes its measure, that is, it's very measurelessness. To think of differ*a*nce in the spirit of Jacques Derrida is to allow the Book to be traversed by the excess of mourning for the death of the other where ethical responsibility to the other is born; it is to expose this Book to the limit that cannot be limited once more; that means, the unheard of limit that is not dialectical. It is to think the impossible: this is what we have learnt, and we have never ceased learning from him, that is: each time we think, decide and form judgment, it has *always already* been traversed by an excess of mourning, by the undecidable, by that which is excess over judgment. And he asks us to be vigilant of the immensity of the abyss of the undecidable each time we assume decision so that justice to the other may be attended and welcomed in 'unconditional hospitality' (Derrida 2000), even before ensuring "my" world and "my" habitation, even beyond the totality of the rational institutions that is established by the power of the negative. Even before Being's comportment to itself, it must always already be opened to the other so that the Book may remain open to the outside; that is: to the movement of writing traversing the Book. Jacques Derrida, like Maurice Blanchot (Blanchot 1995 &1992) calls this space of writing—this space of the outside—as *literature*: literature is the space of the outside that exceeds philosophy's self-presence; the space of the neuter where the "I" disappears without return. Thus Blanchot writes of this neuter-space of literature where negativity is not the task:

> There must always be at least two languages, or two requirements: one dialectical, the other not; one where negativity is the task, the other where the neutral remains apart, cut off both from being and from not-being. In the same way each of us ought both to be a free and speaking subject, and to disappear as passive, patient—the patient whom dying traverses and who does not show himself. (Blanchot 1995: 20).

Literature for Blanchot is the space of the interminable dying without work and without concept, the incessant that stretches itself to the irrecuparable past and un-anticipatable future, beyond the *retention* of a lost time and beyond the *protention* of the coming. As such, literature cannot be reduced to any phenomenological ontology of presence: opening itself beyond all self-presence, literature can only be thought as—as what Michel Foucault refers to as—'the thought of the outside' (Foucault 1989). The logic—which is beyond all logic—of differ*a*nce, is that of an excess of mourning: mourning is that which escapes the Book, and hence, is non-contemporaneous with the Book. At the origin of the Book lies is a mourning which never belongs to the Book. It is perhaps what the tragic poets attempt to evoke, and they are banished by the philosopher for that reason.

The tympan

We will now examine a little text called *Tympan* which is the introduction to Derrida's *Margins—of Philosophy* and we will examine what pertains to the question of the limit and literature's unforeseen intervention or contamination into the Book of philosophy. We will see that to philosophize is not only to tympanize but also to tympanize philosophy: they are non-simultaneous and yet without dialectical opposition and resolution. In other words, to tympanize philosophy is to expose the operation of *Aufhebung* to the non-simultaneity of the two limits (dialectical and the other)—that Blanchot calls "two languages"—so that the Book's inscription is traversed by an excessive sound of the eardrum. The non-simultaneity of the two limits is exposed by Derrida here by exposing the non-simultaneity of the very sense of 'tympan': while to 'tympan' is to inscribe, to print or type 'within' so as to envelop (one of the ways of mastering or appropriating the other, or its limit) and inscribe its closure, it also means to be traversed by the sound of the timbre or to be battered by Vestibular cavity, or eardrum by the sound of the hammer beating. And we know to whom the hammer belongs: to Zarathustra who announces that God is dead, and we also know that Dionysus has small ears. How all this to be understood? To tympanize in French means 'to criticize' philosophy, or, rather, this is what we are asking, it means to push philosophy to the limit that does not have *Aufhebung* for Being-at-the-limit. To tympanize the Book—the Book of philosophy—is to expose the Vestibular cavity of the Book, to expose the eardrum of the Book to the gondola, to the song of melancholy and of mourning, played in timbrel that batters the philosophy's ear:

> Tympan: (1) a timbrel, a drum, (2) inscription, some kind of printing, or writing, (3) any membrane like part of an apparatus, eardrum, Vestibular cavity, leading to the inner recesses whose orifice 1s difficult to find, (4) related to above : "genital vestibule, the vulva and all its parts up to the membrane of hymen exclusively. Also the name of the triangular space limited in front and laterally by the ailerons of the nymphs (small lips of the vulva), and in back by the orifice of the urethra; one enters through this space in practicing Vestibular incision", (5) in architecture: tympanum, triangular space between cornices on the inclined and the horizontal; (6) a stringed musical instrument that has a bow (Derrida 1991: 137).

For Hegel—we refer here to his chapter on "Sense-Certainty" in his *Phenomenology of Spirit*—the system or the Book is the accomplished by the work of death where the universal history realizes itself by the work of negation of the particulars[4]. Here Hegelian onto-theology[5] assumes the task of an "onto-typology"[6]. To the production of the Book belongs, or rather itself is this labour of tympan which is the work of death, on the one hand; and is at the service of the philosophical closure. The task of tympan is to annul in a dialectical manner the oppositions between inside and outside for whose sake Being sets itself to its limit (as our quote from Hegel at the very beginning of this paper shows). To tympanize is for Hegel to posit its limit so as to re-appropriate this very limit: the philosophical eardrum hears only its own music, enclosed within the closure of its Vestibular cavity, deaf to the cry of the other to which Derrida calls phonocentricism (Derrida 1973). With this the Book constitutes its innermost dwelling where the narcissist Being shelters itself from the Siren's song. Hegel's tympan is the economic discourse that hears itself resounding in very depth of its cavity. What it economizes if not the very excess of mourning that from Plato onwards constitutes the very possibility of Philosophy as such? Hegel economizes mourning by making outside the mirror-reflection of the inside—which means positing its limit, its outside, its other so as to cancel this very limit so that no remnant of the outside, no trace of the other would remain un-sublated. Totality is thus accomplished. How to unbalance this economy of representation so that tympan, instead of annulling the other exceeds the very representational order of the circular reappropriation so that tympan, the Vestibular membrane does not make the infinite identity of the outside and inside possible? This is what Derrida asks in this text:

> Under what conditions, then, could one mark for a philosopheme in general, a limit, a margin that it could not infinitely re-appropriable, conceive as its own, in advance engendering and interning the process of its expropriation (Hegel again, always) proceeding to its inversion by itself? How to unbalance the pressure that corresponds to each other on either side of the membrane'? ...How to interpret—but here interpretation can no longer be a theory or discursive practice of philosophy—the strange and unique property of a discourse that organizes the economy of its representation, the law of its proper weave, such that its outside is never its outside, never surprises it, such that the logic of its heteronomy still reasons from within the vault of its autism. (Derrida 1991: 154-55).

To *tympanize* philosophy—and not that of philosophy tympanizing—is to unbalance the inside and the outside when the outside is not nothing but a traversal that overflows the Vestibular cavity of the Book, that opens to the outside wailing and mourning when Socrates drank poison. Can we call this outside—which is neither a concept nor a proper name—literature? Literature is this wound that opens itself to the melancholic song of the gondola which Zarathustra sang, played in tympan. To *tympanize*—this unheard tympan, not of the Book and is thus otherwise than inscription of death—to tympanize is to make Socrates practice music, as Nietzsche desires (Nietzsche 1996: 93), the music of infinite mourning of Dionysian tragedy so that the eardrum of the Book is tympanized and is exposed to the infinity of dying beyond return.

It appears as if 'tympan', this single word—what a strange word is this!—opens itself beyond the economy of the Book to another tympan, another limit as passage traversing the Book's very limit. It appears as if the Book's closure is inhabited by other music, unbeknownst to itself. Like Nietzsche desiring Socrates to play music, perhaps Derrida too desires Hegel practice music so that Hegel's eardrum is attuned to the mourning of the other's dying. The strange relationship between philosophy and literature is this non-co-relation of two tympans, two modalities of thinking death and two incommensurable limits.

The haunting of writing

What mourning has to do with 'tympan'? For Hegel mourning is the origin of the Book: to inscribe or to tympanize is to annihilate the sense-certainty of "this" or "that". The mourning for this violence that opens the space for universal history constitutes the very inscription of the Book of history that Hegel recounts in *Phenomenology of Spirit* (in the manner that the loss of the name in its immediateness constitutes the structure of naming, in the sense that the act of naming annihilates the "thing" it designates)[7]. But the Book is also the atonement, or rather *catharsis*—*catharsis* in the speculative sense—of mourning and of violence in the sense that through the annihilation of the "thing" in its sensuous character gives birth to the ideality of the thing in its universal essence. In signification the thing (in the immediateness of its sensuous appearance) dies away, but the ideality of sense appears which for Hegel is the universal properly where the thing annihilated is resurrected: 'the speculative Good Friday' (Hegel 1977: 191). The Book or system (of universal history) is originary event of violence, but this violence is atoned on the 'speculative Good Friday' at the closure of the Book: mourning is thus vainly (and supposedly) consoled, meaning is saved and discourse becomes possible. Hegel who himself knew this deep, unappeasable melancholy all through his own life, also sought to economize this abyss of melancholy by inscribing it within his System or Book only as mere moment. As if hereby on this 'speculative Good Friday' Hegel has turned the disease itself into remedy: a truly *cathartic* moment, by a truly homeopathic treatment. By employing death into the work for the sake of universal history, he sought to evade the other death—that is, death that does not work, the "worklessness" of death as Blanchot used to say (Blanchot 1995), death that is without concept and without name, death that cannot be elevated into the ideality of signification. By tympanizing death, Hegel could evade the 'poisonous sting' (Rosenzweig 2005: 9) of the other death; by economizing the limit into just the limit between two concepts, he sought to evade the limit that cannot be maintained, limit that cannot be looked in its eye. The result is the cowardly gesture of philosophy: there is the Book that only has to murmur ceaselessly its own song.

But is it not that the event of violence at the origin of the Book is *always already* traversed by another violence that refuses to be idealized into universal signification? It seems that the beginning of the Book is *always already* traversed by amore originary violence that is without concept and without name, of which Derrida calls *arché-violence*. Alluding to Rousseau here, Derrida says:

> For writing, obliteration of the proper classed in the play of difference, is the originary violence itself: pure impossibility of the "vocative mark", impossible purity of the mark of vocation. This "equivocation" which Rousseau hoped would be eliminated by a "vocative mark" " cannot be effaced. For the existence of such a mark in any code of punctuation would not change the problem. The death of the absolutely proper naming, recognizing in a language the other as pure other, invoking it as what it is, is the death of the pure idiom reserved for the unique. Anterior to the possibility of violence ...there is as space of possibility, the violence

of the arché-writing, the violence of difference, of classification and of the system of appellations. (Derrida 1994: 110).

Even before mourning for the annihilation of the sensuous objects which would be elevated into the ideality of signification there lays the *arché-violence*: that is, naming that inhibits, prohibits the pure appearance of the other as other. Thus the violence to the other is more originary than the sacrifice of one's own empirical being for the sake of the universality of signification. The more originary violence against the other lies in that, to speak with Levinas, the other cannot be sacrificed, that the other is un-sacrificiable. It is from Derrida, and also from Maurice Blanchot and Emmanuel Levinas that we have learnt to think the other death, the other who cannot be killed and who is unsacrificiable. From Maurice Blanchot we have learnt to think of this "worklessness" of dying beyond the closure of the Book of philosophy as literature. If Derrida has asked us to be attentive to this other dying that cannot be thought within the closure of the Book, that is in so far as the infinite movement of writing opens itself beyond the closure of the Book in an infinite responsibility to the other who is unsacrificiable. If to think the non-philosophical is an ethical task, the question of literature is this very question of the ethical responsibility to the infinite other. It is not that literature survives intact after the demise of philosophy but rather this: what persists beyond the death of philosophy is what we call "literature" which is neither a persistence of being nor essence but an interminability of its dying that knows no concept and no name. It is in so far as literature is *always already* dying even before the birth of the ideality of signification, and that it would not stop dying even after the death of philosophy.

NOTES

1. Thus Hegel says in *Phenomenology of Spirit*: 'Death, if that is what we want to call this non-actuality, is of all things the most dreaded and to hold fast what is dead requires the greatest strength…but the

life of the Spirit is not the life that shrinks from death and keeps itself untouched by devastation, but rather the life that endures it and maintains itself in it. It wins its truth only when, in utter dismemberment, it finds itself. It is this power, not as something positive, which closes its eyes to the negative, as when we say of something that it is nothing or is false, and then, having done with it, turn away and pass onto something else; on the contrary, Spirit is this power only by looking negative in the face and tarrying with it (Hegel 1998: 19).

2. It is Emmanuel Levinas, more than any other contemporary philosopher, who keeps returning, almost in an obsessive manner, to the event character of death in its advent from the extremity of time, that is, from the pure future to which no mastery of a subject or being, and no phenomenology of the eidetic consciousness can attain thematisation. The mortal's relation to death is not that of virility or mastery, but a 'reversal of the subject's activity into passivity' (Levinas 1987: 72). As such, the phenomenon of death, which is not a phenomenon like others, is the very relation to the event of the unknown: 'here an event can happen to us that we no longer assume, not even in the way we assume events—because we are always immersed in the empirical world—through vision' (ibid: 74). He goes onto say: 'this event as mystery, precisely because it could not be anticipated—that is, grasped; it could not enter into a presence or it could enter into it as what does not enter it' (Ibid: 77).
3. It is this relation of death to responsibility that brings together, despite their irreducible singularities, the thoughts of Jacques Derrida and Emmanuel Levinas. I refer to Levinas' lectures on *God, Death and Time* (Levinas 2000).
4. Thus Hegel writes: 'It is the power of speech, as that which performs what has to be performed. For it is the real existence of the pure self as self; in speech, self-consciousness, *qua independent separate individuality*, comes as such into existence, so that it exists for others...language, however, contains it in its purity, it alone expresses the "I" the "I" itself. This *real* existence of the "I" is *qua* real existence, an objectivity which has in it the true nature of the "I". The "I" is this particular "I"—but equally the *universal* "I"; its

manifesting is also at once the externalisation and vanishing of *this* particular "I", and as a result the "I" remains in its universality. The "I" that utters itself is *heard* or *perceived*; it is an infection in which it has immediately passed into unity with those for whom it is a real existence, and is a universal self-consciousness. That it is *perceived* or *heard* means that *its real existence dies away*; this its otherness has been taken back into itself; and its real existence is just this: that as a self-conscious Now, as real existence, it is *not* a real existence, and through this vanishing it *is* a real existence' (Hegel 1998: 308-09).

5. For explication of Hegel's metaphysics of onto-theology, see Heidegger's discussion in "The Onto-theological Constitution of Metaphysics" (Heidegger 1969).
6. Also see Lacoue-Labarthe's remarkable discussion on the relation between the ontological notion of *Gestalt* and typing (Lacoue-Labarthe 1998).
7. See Alexander Kojeve's lectures on Hegel that is collected together as *Introduction to the Reading of Hegel* (Kojeve 1980).

REFERENCES

Bataille, Georges, "Hegel, Death and Sacrifice" and "Letter to X, Lecturer on Hegel" in *The Bataille Reader*, ed. Fred Botting and Scott Wilson (Oxford: Blackwell, 1997), pp. 279-300.

Beckett, Samuel, *The Three Novels: Molloy, Malone Dies, The Unnamable* (New York: Grove Press, 1994).

Blanchot, Maurice, *The Writing of the Disaster,* trans. Ann Smock (Lincoln: University of Nebraska Press, 1995).

Blanchot, Maurice, *The Step Not Beyond,* trans. Lycette Nelson (Albany: State University of New York Press, 1992).

Derrida, Jacques and Anne Doufourmantelle, *Of Hospitality,* trans. Rachel Bowlby (Stanford: Stanford University Press, 2000).

Derrida, Jacques, *Of Grammatology,* trans. Gayatri Chakravorty Spivak (Delhi: Motilal Benarasidass, 1994).

Derrida, Jacques, "Tympan" in *A Derrida Reader: Between the Blinds*, ed. Peggy Kamuf (New York: Columbia University Press, 1991).

Derrida, Jacques, *Speech and Phenomenon: And Other Essays on Husserl's Theory of Signs,* trans. David W. Allison (Evanston: Northwestern University Press, 1973).

Foucault/Blanchot, *The Thought from Outside* and *Michel Foucault as I imagine Him,* trans. Jeffrey Mehlman and Brian Massumi (New York: Zone Books, 1989).

Hegel, G.W.F, *Phenomenology of Spirit,* trans. A.V. Miller (New Delhi: Motilal Banarasidass, 1998).

Hegel, G.W.F., *Faith and Knowledge,* trans. Walter Cerf and H.S Harris (Albany: State University of New York, 1977).

Hegel, G.W.F., *Logic,* trans. William Wallace (Oxford: Clarendon Press, 1975).

Heidegger, Martin, *Identity and Difference,* trans. Joan Stambaugh (New York: Harper & Row, 1969).

Heidegger, Martin, *Being and Time,* trans. John Macquarrie and Edward Robinson (New York: Harper & Row, 1962).

Kojeve, Alexander, *Introduction to the Reading of Hegel: Lectures on the Phenomenology of Spirit,* ed. Allan Bloom and trans. James H. Nichols, Jr. (Cornell: Cornell University Press, 1980).

Lacoue-Labarthe, Philippe, *Typography: Mimesis, Philosophy, Politics,* ed. Christopher Fynsk (Stanford, California: Stanford University Press, 1998).

Levinas, Emmanuel, *God, Death and Time,* trans. Bettino Bergo (Stanford: Stanford University Press, 2000).

Levinas, Emmanuel, *Time and the Other,* trans. Richard A Cohen (Pittsburgh & Pennsylvania: Duquesne University Press, 1987).

Nietzsche, Friedrich, *Thus Spoke Zarathustra,* trans. Walter Kaufmann (New York: Modern Library, 1995).

Nietzsche, Friedrich, *The Birth of Tragedy* and *The Case of Wagner,* trans. Walter Kaufmann (New York: Vintage Books, 1996).

Rosenzweig, Franz, *The Star of Redemption,* trans. Barbara E. Galli (Wisconsin: The University of Wisconsin Press, 2005).

The abyss of human freedom

This paper attempts to examine Martin Heidegger's analysis of the question of freedom in his lecture course on *The Essence of Human Freedom*. Taking Heidegger's deconstructive reading of Kant as point of departure, this paper in a Heideggerian manner attempts to think freedom in a more originary manner : not as man's property, but the unconditional opening, or the possibility of existence itself as such. In this sense freedom is the very event of the possibility of existence itself which breaks through in the mortal being. The human grounded in this manner in freedom is open to the ground of his own existence in so far as he is the most finite of all beings. Finitude is thus not an impossibility of freedom but the very possibility of existence itself. Freedom is no longer thought here as the human's will to determine itself on its own ground, but freedom as the very groundless site of history's inauguration and is thus irreducible to any causality, whether transcendental causality or practical causality of Kantian type. As the very groundless condition of the mortal's event of existence, freedom is not one question of amongst others but the very question of finitude itself out of which existence erupts. This event of freedom, thus understood, is the event of *leap* from the grounding principle of reason, even if it is practical reason and the principle of causality to the un-groundable event of inauguration of finite history itself.

The no-thing of freedom and the finitude of the human

> Human freedom now no longer means freedom as a property of man, but *man as a possibility of freedom*. Human freedom is the freedom that breaks through in man and takes him up into itself, thus making man possible. If freedom is the ground of the possibility of understanding being in its whole breath and fullness, then man, as *grounded* in his existence upon and *in this* freedom is the site where beings *in* the whole become revealed, i.e. he is that particular being *through which being as such announce themselves.*
>
> —Martin Heidegger (2005: 94-95)

Any attempt to think freedom essentially must begin with the *spacing*, or *opening* that is opened by the works of Martin Heidegger. Heidegger gives himself the task of thinking freedom in a way which is free from the systemic task of freedom. If in the dominant metaphysical tradition of the West freedom is understood as ideals of reason, of ground and foundation of being (that is, from onto-theology of any type), or understood in its own specific, non-phenomenal causality irreducible to any cognitive or conceptual determination, or even understood as the free will of the human(as if freedom were man's property), in Heidegger's deconstruction of the dominant metaphysics of subjectivity and foundation we find a space of freedom that first of all opens, manifests, reveals, un-conceals the world and the entirety of existence to the mortals on the basis of his essential finitude, that means, on the basis of a non-basis, groundless, abyss, impossibility, or the limit. *Thus for Heidegger freedom is no longer reason as the self-grounding act or self-unifying act on the basis of the metaphysics of subjectivity, but rather is the very event of existence as such.* Thus the *facticity* of existence itself is nothing other than that which arises out of the ground of the *facticity* of freedom itself: *freedom's existence is first of all a fact.* This *facticity* exposes Dasein toward its own nothingness, to its own impossibility and groundlessness, towards the event of closure that at once releases this closure to its impossible, namely, its inalienable finitude. Therefore for

Dasein, as Heidegger recounts in *Being and Time,* death always appears as an unenclosed futurity, even at the very moment of its imminent arrival, insofar as it presents itself as, or appears itself as impossibility, as no-thing, as non-phenomenal arriving, a non-present presentation, precisely because death presents itself purely without reserve. If the existentiality of Dasein is the existence concerns, not so much with any given presence (*Vorhandenheit)* but with the event of a non-phenomenal arriving, then this free opening is none but the very thought of futurity of existence, of existence in its *event-character* insofar as Dasein's existence is *always already* a "to-come" (where we must understand this *coming* in the infinitude of its verbal resonance and not in the manner of *Vorhandenheit,* that is, of 'the entities presently given'). Insofar as Dasein is not to be understood as the metaphysical subjectivity and therefore, its essence is not the essence of acting and positing, Dasein as no-thing is to be distinguished from the negativity of a dialectical-speculative nature. This non-thing is none other than no-thing of freedom itself, of freedom that is an inapparent apparition that cannot be thought in terms of a 'this' or 'that' thing, but as this *coming* itself.

Therefore the apparition of freedom does not occur amongst the entities of the given world. In his lecture on *What is Metaphysics*? Heidegger therefore distinguishes the Not of a nothingness from the Not of negativity (Heidegger 1998: 82-96). The manifestation of nothing in relation to which alone freedom manifests itself to the mortal existence (that Dasein is) is more originary than the annihilation-character of the negativity. This means: the abyss of freedom cannot be measured by negativity; only the originary nothingness can measure up to freedom only so far as the essence of this measure consists in its *transcendence* of all measure, or, rather, the nothingness is always already the originary measure of all measures (hence is the immeasurable par excellence). This measure is the measure of *transcendence* insofar Dasein who is called upon to assume its very existence (out of its finitude) by freedom, itself is that being that *always already* transcends any mode of entitative presence. Taking this point from Heidegger we can further speak of the possibility of existence itself as such: that there is the world, personality and self only because they are the *donation* of the immeasurable: the immeasurable that appears itself as nothingness without annihilating anything. The measure of transcendence—the very measure of freedom—is not something lying outside the beings as a whole, but that which manifests itself in the appearing of the beings as a whole in the receding of beings, in their very withdrawal and abandonment. This is only in so far as Dasein itself is not an entity presently given nor an object with animated freewill at disposal, a *Zoë* somehow got attached with *Bio,* but because Dasein itself is the free *spacing* or opening which opens itself to the Nothing (where beings as a whole manifests itself in the movement of withdrawal and abandonment). In his *What is Metaphysics*? Heidegger speaks of this holding out into the open as *transcendence*,

> *Dasein means: being held into the nothing.*
>
> Holding itself out in the nothing, Dasein is in each case already beyond beings as a whole. Such being beyond beings we call *transcendence*. If in the ground of its essence Dasein were not transcending, which now means, if it were not in advance holding itself out into the nothing; then it could never adopt a stance toward beings nor even toward itself.
>
> Without the original manifestness of the nothing, no selfhood and no freedom (Ibid: 91).

Freedom manifests itself on the basis of the manifestation of nothing, which is none but the very appearing of being in its withdrawal and abandonment. Heidegger thought this double, agonistic character of revealing and receding of beings as a whole in its donation and abandonment, a revealing that makes manifest to us a deeper, far reaching and the abyssal character of freedom. Freedom is that which granting the possibility of existence, withdraws and recedes from all phenomenal appearing. What is implicit in this text of Heidegger—that is, the unthought in thought—is the abyssal-agonistic manifestation of freedom: that arising of freedom out of the groundless of the nothing, agonistically and in the manner of *strife* between Day and Night, life and Death that Heraclitus speaks of, the strife that gives and withdraws, manifests and recedes at the same time, and thereby copulating the elements in a monstrous-agonal manner that Hölderlin speaks of: the arising of the wholly otherwise precisely at the moment when history pauses absolutely; that moment which while revealing the whole of history in an absolute presentation, also reveals to us the receding of the whole of history. It thereby yawns open the void precisely at the moment of its accomplishment, in its plenitude and fulfillment. If freedom is nothing else but the principle of inauguration and of inception, then freedom reveals itself here at this moment, each time as absolutely first before everything else. *History inaugurates with freedom, granted by freedom.*

The ethico-political task of thinking of our time therefore must take the question of finitude seriously, insofar as what remains for us the sense of ethico-political is none but that of finitude of itself. Our sense of the ethico-political—that means, our sense of the world—demands that we maintain this impossible tie with the agony and strife of freedom itself, to assume the risk that freedom opens us to, and to assume the task of this very assumption, that of the *leap* from givenness of immanence to the holding sway of being . To minimize this wager of freedom and of its agony and strife through various programmatic and calculative apparatus of modern technological reason would be to deny the very principle of inauguration on the basis of which our sense of the ethico-political rests. This is what the Heideggerian thought has opened for us and with which we must begin here (taking care of what is at stake in Heideggerian thought of freedom as event in its intrinsic relation with the groundlessness). The transcendence of this finitude is a constant and interminable wager out of which there arises the possibility of invention of a new ethics and new politics, for what we want to understand here by "the political" is the agonal manifestation of freedom. This agonal manifestation of freedom and its irreducible strife cannot be reducible to the dialectical oppositions of principles with its *Aufhebung*.

To come to Heidegger, the thought of the care for Dasein now, after so many years of Heidegger's speaking of it, makes sense for us only because it gives us the thought of a freedom free from all immanent totalization. To understand the sense of freedom as wager is to understand first of all our ethics and our politics itself as wager. This is only so far as the wager of freedom is none other than freedom as strife: the agonal manifestation of differential partitioning of forces. As such, the question of freedom concerns the very possibility of human existence itself: the human is of all beings the most awesome because he is the most finite of all beings. He is this possibility to openness to the whole of beings only insofar as he is essentially this being, inextricably finite and inalienably mortal. This mortal's openness to the world and to the futurity happens not out of mortal's free will to determine itself on its own ground, but out of a groundless essence of freedom itself.

Causality as a problem of freedom

Heidegger's lecture on *The Essence of Human Freedom* is his most systematic attempt to understand the enigmatic question of freedom. Taking Kant's grounding of freedom as a problematic of causality as its point of departure—in its twofold *transcendental freedom* and *practical freedom*—Heidegger attempts to think freedom in a more originary manner: not freedom as a problematic of causality, but rather the causality as a problematic of freedom.

If Heideggerian attempt to think of causality as a problem of freedom and not vice versa is taken into account, then freedom can neither be understood merely as the principle of inauguration that inaugurates the series of events and occurrences (and thus as mere extension of causality) nor freedom be understood as practical reason of the finite being in relation to his pure will willing itself. Freedom would then has to be understood in a more originary manner as the ground of the being (which is *Abgrund*) which means the possibility of existence as such on the basis of which alone there may be willing of the pure will (so that this finite being determines itself as self-determining personality). Freedom is the site where the events occur as such in their multiple singularities, but this multiplicity of events does not occur as temporal succession of nows. Following Heidegger, we are no longer understanding events here as particular homogenous occurrences where the relation of discontinuity between events belongs to the causal sequence. What we want to think with Heidegger is something that has remained not so explicitly brought out in Heidegger himself, in so far as Heidegger's deconstruction of Kant's notion of causality has remained (at least in this lecture course) in the giving over causality to the site of freedom. What we want to understand, taking Heidegger's controversy with Kant as point of departure, is this radical notion of *the event* that does not yet belong to the temporal, relative succession of occurrences, events that are no longer the relative, sequential, accumulative, homogenous discontinuity of occurrences which point to the absolute spontaneity that begins with itself (only because it does not have to regress or progress *ad-infinitum*). What we want to learn from Heidegger is rather the possibility of the event that inaugurates absolutely, that means without ground and foundation, is yet universal: this universality is in turn no longer to be thought as the accumulative totality of present particular instances that are to follow in their letting-follow in a temporal-causal sequence; nor the universal here is to be understood as the will purely determining itself in a time before time; the universal is rather to be understood as that which arrives each such letting-follow as from an outside, not merely regulating the sequence as a regulative principle, but de-formalizing the sequence each time it arrives absolutely.

It is this pure arrival that we want to call *the event*: it is not an occurrence that belongs to the sequential order of letting-follow or just running-ahead of only because it does not adequately express the universality of the moral law. What we want to think, in this name "the event" neither belongs to the universality of the moral law nor to the universality of the dialectical-speculative history, nor even to a mere instantiation of the universality in the particular eruption of 'now' that follow other nows in a sequence forming a uniform procession or progression. What we call "the event" is rather the de-formalization of any such a sequential progression, which erupting in an irreducibly singular manner, nevertheless is an inscription of universality. Such idiomatic universality—or, singular universality—is a disruption of the immanence of the formal temporality (the latter is only accomplished through visible, apparent forms of phenomenality). Such an event is to be understood in its exemplarity. This exemplarity of the event is the inscription of universality in the singular, where the immanence of particulars instants of eruption forming a causal chain is hollowed inside out, thus exposed to the transcendence of the wholly other.

This thought is already implicit in Heidegger's deconstruction of Kant's notion of freedom when, for example, Heidegger speaks of freedom as the ground of the possibility of event as such. Here it would have been possible for him to distinguish at that time between *occurrence* and *the event of arrival.* Then it would have either the particular occurrences belonging to the temporal sequence in their letting-follow, or, the irreducible universal moral law in particular instantiation of it in willing *this* or *that.* But what has opened by Heidegger in this work on human freedom is the question concerning the grounding of the will of the human in relation to his finitude, in the *Abgrund* of the ground, so that freedom comes to be seen (by Heidegger) as the very possibility of existence of Dasein which is irreducible either to transcendental freedom or to practical freedom. Instead, both the transcendental freedom and the practical freedom are to be opened up to the *Abgrund:* to that the abyss of freedom which is the possibility of the finite existence of the mortal. Thus causality (as one ontological determination of beings among others) belongs to freedom which alone is the condition of the manifestation of beings. Heidegger could say:

> Causality is, however, *one* ontological determination of beings among others.
>
> *Causality is grounded in freedom. The problem of causality is a problem of freedom and not vice versa* (Heidegger 2005: 207)

Thus the inaugurating principle of freedom is no longer merely that of inaugurating the series of occurrences in a temporal-causal succession, nor the inaugurating a series of ethical actions as the will that purely determines itself, *but inauguration of the very possibility of the occurrence of existence as such and of the mortal who thus arises out of freedom. Manifestation of beings: the event of freedom!* What Heidegger here attempts to understand is the event character of freedom which is the manifestation of being on the basis of which alone can there be the causality, and can there at all be inauguration of the series of sequential occurrences. That means freedom cannot be understood on the basis of causality; freedom is what is presupposed in any causality as the unconditioned opening and revealing of beings. The event of freedom is then no longer to be understood on the basis of given presence, or as the constant presence, but *coming into presence* which is irreducible to any given presence or constant presence. Heidegger here is clear in this point:

> As a category, causality is a basic character of the being of beings. If we consider that the being of beings is proximally comprehended as constant presence—and this involves producedness, producing finishing in the broad sense of actualizing—it is clear that precisely *causality,* in the traditional sense of the being of beings, in common understanding as in the traditional metaphysics, is the *fundamental category of being as being-present.* If *causality is a problem of freedom* and not vice versa then the *problem of being in general* is in itself *a problem of freedom* (Ibid: 205-06).

What is presupposed in the dominant, traditional metaphysical understanding of causality is a certain determination of time as given present, as constant presence. What Heidegger here attempts to problematize by reading deconstructively Kant's notion of freedom is to be traced back to the concerns of *Being and Time*. In Kant as in the traditional, dominant metaphysical determination of Being, Being is understood on the basis of the reductive-derivative understanding of time as constant present, as given present which has remained unquestioned. Kant understands freedom as a problematic of causality. This causality presupposes the dominant, metaphysical determination of beings as 'entities given present' (*Vorhandenheit*) which in turn tactically presupposes the vulgar notion of time as constant presence which can be categorically grasped in the predicative determination (that means, *apophantically*). What has there remained unthought is the very event of *coming* itself—not *this* or *that* coming, nor the occurrences that can be arranged in causal- temporal succession of homogenous instants, but—that arises groundlessly out of the abyss of freedom. *The event of coming then can no longer be understood as a conditioned arriving, but since it occurs freely, that means unconditionally, it can never be thought on the basis of causality*. Therefore the dominant, traditional, metaphysical understanding of the event on the basis of the understanding of time as constant present that can be arranged on a causal scale of various attenuated, accumulative, homogenous instants (*nows*) is inadequate to grasp the event of freedom that erupts incalculably and unpredictably. This event of freedom arrests the homogenous march of history and brings it to a sudden standstill. Here time would then thought in a disjunctive simultaneity that inaugurates history itself anew which cannot be reduced to the inauguration of new series of the causal chain of temporal instants. Since this abyss of the event of time (which is the very event of freedom) does not present itself in any self-presence, its unapparent apparition can only be that of an infinite *coming*, a *transcendence without transcendent*. This transcendence of freedom is the very moment of history is *coming to presence* as if for the first time (which defines the historicity of history) which is not the occurrences within a causal chain of succession, nor does it belong to a scale that assimilates the sequential, periodic, attenuated, relative discontinuities; it is rather the moment of radical arriving when the whole sequence comes to standstill. What we learn from Heidegger's deconstructive reading of the dominant metaphysical determination of freedom is this thought of the infinity of freedom as the event of pure arrival, of history is *coming into presence* to itself.

Philosophy as strife

If philosophy is concerned not with *this* or *that* mode of presently given entities (or, with *this* or *that* area of the presently given entities) but the very *coming to presence* of existence itself *as such*, then philosophy cannot be reduced to be one amongst other academic disciplines: philosophy should be understood as the event of thinking the unconditional that erupts out of no-thing of freedom itself. From where, then, the name "philosophy" is to be derived? As if, as it were, this strange name "philosophy"—erupting out of no-thing and no-ground—can only be the name of a thinking from such an Archimedean point of the unnamable and non-condition. In other words, philosophy is such a state of exception in relation to the presently given mode of existence in the world, and in such a manner that philosophy, instead of merely and thus only relatively re- working the presently given mode of existence in the world, seeks rather the complete transformation of the world as an epochal inauguration arising together with the epochal break. The poet Hölderlin speaks of this event as 'the monstrous copulation' (Hölderlin 1988: 96-100). Philosophy, wherever it occurs, appears as an inauguration of an entirely new relation to the world; or rather, the world *happens there*, in the open site of freedom, as if for the first time. This occurring of the world—or, let us say, the *worlding* of the world from where alone we mortals derive our sense of the world—constitutes the event of the world. This event of the world occurrence, which inaugurates an entirely new relation to the world, is no longer a merely reworking the given mode of existence: it cannot be understood as mere an occurrence of causality. It is the event of freedom itself, arising out of freedom, whose ungrounded condition is freedom. While referring to Schelling's notion of philosophy as an event of freedom, Heidegger refers to philosophy and poetry, wherever they occur, as world occurrences:

> Where they are essential, thinking and writing poetry are a *world occurrence*, and this is not only in the sense that something is happening within the world which has significance for the world, but also in the sense in which and through which the world itself arises itself anew in its actual origins and rules as world. Philosophy can never be justified by taking over and reworking the realm what is knowable from some areas or even all areas and delivering things that knowable from this, but only by opening more primordially the essence of the *truth* of what is knowable and discoverable in general and giving a *new path* and a *new horizon* to the relation to the beings in general. (Heidegger 1985: 58)

What is thought as philosophy is what is essential in philosophy: *philosophy that welcomes the pure taking place of the world, rather than merely knowledge of the given world.* As such, it is not concerned with *this* or *that* conditioned presence; it rather welcomes the unconditional in pure *coming* as such. Philosophy, since it is the work of freedom, does not concern itself with naming the nameable, but naming the unnamable and the un-naming the nameable. Philosophy in this manner, again, manifests the strife of freedom: philosophy manifests itself as the agonal manifestation of the nameable and unnamable, the condition and unconditional, joy and mourning at the same time, in a disjunctive constellation. Philosophy as such is essentially aporetic: not between the condition and another condition, not between a name and another, or even less, between a concept and another concept, but rather: between the conditioned and the unconditioned, both at once, as wager. Each time there is philosophy lies there a risk, a madness, or even impossibility, insofar as it is demanded as the task of philosophy which arises out of freedom that, on the one hand it must the name the unnamable (so that philosophy constantly confronts the enigma of its own disappearing at the very moment of its fulfillment), and other hand, that the unnamable must remain irreducible to each and everything in the world that is named and predicated (so that it can welcome, unconditionally, what is *not yet*, and what is pure taking place of the event). This is insofar as freedom itself calls forth its other in an agonistic manner, in the manner of strife: the *necessity* to which it holds itself by being separated from the other, like the elements of strife in Heraclitus. Thus when Schelling (1936) refers to the contradiction of necessity and freedom (which is a higher form of contradiction than between spirit and nature), he is alluding precisely to the highest agonistic elements of philosophy itself: the strife between the condition and the unconditioned, the disappearance and the arriving, the inapparition and the apparition of freedom itself. This agony of strife, while animating the very movement of philosophy each time when philosophy announces itself, remains inapparent to the eyes of the world. It is, in other words, a secret. Referring to this strife that arises out of philosophy or philosophy itself as this strife, Heidegger says:

> Philosophy is intrinsically a strife between necessity and freedom and in that it belongs to philosophy as the highest knowledge to know itself, it will produce from itself this strife and thus the question of the system of freedom. (Heidegger 1985: 58).

REFERENCES

Heidegger, Martin, *The Essence of Human Freedom*, trans. Ted Sadler (London, New York: Continuum, 2005)

Heidegger, Martin, *Schelling's Treatise on the Essence of Human Freedom*, trans. Joan Stambaugh (Athens: Ohio University Press, 1985)

Heidegger, Martin, 'What is Metaphysics?', in *Pathmarks*, trans. William McNeill (Cambridge: Cambridge University Press, 1998), pp. 82-96.

Hölderlin, Friedrich, 'Becoming in Dissolution' in *Essays and Letters on Theory,* trans. Thomas Pfau (Albany, State University New York Press, 1988), pp. 96-100.

Schelling, F.W.J. von, *Philosophical Inquiries into the Nature of Human Freedom,* trans. James Gutmann (La Salle: Illinois, 1936 and 1992).

Wholly otherwise

The notion of messianic time seems to evoke an aporia that refuses dialectical resolution with *Aufhebung* as the operative concept of a speculative-dialectical determination of historical time—the messianic aporia that is how to think of messianic coming which is here and now, a future arriving which is, at the same time, a here and now. This demands a rigor of thinking that ventures beyond the dialectical aporia to think of an *existential* coming, irreducible to the predicative determination that is intimately tied to the metaphysical thinking of language guided by the logical notion of judgment. This article takes Schelling's notion of *Scheidung*—meaning both "de-cision" and "cision"—to consider a coming beyond the predicative process of dialectical history. Hence, the de-cision, which is the cision of ground and existence as a non-conditional opening for the coming *to* presence, cannot be thought of on the basis of *Aufhebung*. It has a relation to a time that falls outside dialectical-speculative time and remains as a remnant, and also points towards the messianic coming of redemption that remains beyond death.

Venturing beyond

> Thinking means venturing beyond. (Bloch 1986: 5)

If thinking is not merely to be saturated with the given, but in its very movement restlessly ventures beyond all that is given, and thereby opens itself to the possible, then this "venturing beyond" would have an essential relation with the wholly otherwise, for the possible—more than the realized—is pregnant with the otherwise, with the possibility of the wholly otherwise. The requirement of thinking about the future, felt nowadays more than ever before, therefore takes seriously the question of the *possible* in relation to the time wholly otherwise, a wholly otherwise time, a wholly otherwise of time.[1] This wholly otherwise time is not the possible time that is actualized without remnant, but rather the *possibility as remnant* so that there remains the possibility of the wholly otherwise. This thinking of a time outside as possible—for the thinking of the possible is also, in an essential manner, a thinking of the outside—has an intimate relation to what Heidegger (1980) calls *Grundstimmung*, the "fundamental mood" or "fundamental attunement" of hope. Hope is hope for the possible, for the coming of the wholly otherwise, to which also belongs—and this is the aporia—the possibility of the coming of the wholly otherwise than hoped. The coming of the wholly otherwise than hoped which belongs to the possibility fills us with melancholy, another "fundamental attunement". This is a melancholy that is not merely over what has been—which is the past—but melancholy in relation to the future, in relation to the possible, for with the possible of the coming of the hoped, the possible of the coming of the unhoped is also given.[2]

It is here that the relation of temporality with mood should be considered more closely. If melancholy has always been determined in the dominant thinking of mood—whether psychoanalysis or otherwise—in relation to a loss in the past that is irrecuparable and not yet redeemed, it is necessary to rethink the relationship of melancholic mood with time, for a melancholy may be felt not only with a loss in the irrevocable past, even though imaginary, but also in the here and now, and also in relation to the possible that is yet *to* come. Thinking, therefore, in "venturing beyond", and in being concerned with the possible and the wholly otherwise, is not only intimated by the fundamental attunement of a *messianic* hope for redemption—which Ernst Bloch calls "the principle of hope" (1986)—but also a fundamental attunement of melancholy. An opening to the *coming*, an opening to an opening, or an opening to the possible and wholly otherwise—which, perhaps, constitutes the ethico-political task for our time—therefore always is intimated by the caesural, aporetic double attunements of hope and melancholy: the unredeemed melancholy requires that time itself be opened to hope for the coming of the Messiah, to the redemptive hope in the possible of the wholly otherwise coming, and since this requirement demands our historico-political labour of realization and actualization, this opening to the possible constitutes the very historico-political task of our time. The aporetic moods of our ethico-political thinking of the future consist in precisely this. The requirement of venturing to the possible not only attunes us to the messianic hope, but also attunes us to the fundamental melancholy at the realization which is always conditioned. Since all realization is only the limitation of the possible and always finite, this melancholy remains unredeemed and calls for ever-remaining hope, hope for the affirmation of the future that remains, a remaining hope in the future of affirmation. This venturing beyond to the possible exceeds each time of the moment of realization here and now and therefore it appears as redemptive. A melancholy at the realization here and now—for the realization at each time of the here and now is only a limitation of the possible and finite—demands a here and now wholly otherwise (than the given), a wholly otherwise of the possible here and now beyond *this* here and now that happened, as if at each moment there comes a here and now, there is already an opening, by an ineluctable logic, to a here and now wholly otherwise, forever incommensurable with the given, heterogeneous to the given, an opening of time itself to hope heterogeneous, and yet inseparable from the melancholy of realization[3]. Thus, the aporetic of the hope and melancholy that constitutes the aporetic of the ethico-political thinking of our time is nothing but an aporia of time itself: an aporia between a here and now that is realized and has arrived on the one hand, and the here and now of the possible and yet to come on the other hand, as if a caesura, a spacing or an interruption opens each towards the other, and thereby separates each from the other.

What is it to think the ethico-political task anew, the messianic task of affirming the yet *to* come, in so far as such a task must traverse an experience of impossibility?

The time messianic

The question of messianic time often arises out of the need to respond to the contradiction which the very notion of "messianic time" seems to evoke: on the one hand, messianic time evokes a time *to* come, a future that has not yet happened; and yet, on the other hand, messianic time is also here and now, the plenitude and fullness of now, a presence overflowing the cup of the presently given. It is the difficulty of affirming this non-dialectical aporia, which—in so far as it is non-dialectical—does not point towards a dialectical sublation (*Aufhebung*) in relation to the synthetic third. If dialectical contradiction is between the non-being and the being[4], the contradiction which we think of in the messianic must be otherwise: in other words, not in relation to the dialectical third of synthesis, which is an immanent possibility in the dialectical process itself, but to the third that does not sublate the two that are given presences, which therefore is yet *to* come. Therefore this notion of *possibility* or *potentiality* as *immanent*, is understood in both Aristotle and Hegel as *hama* (see Derrida 1982), which means *simul*: the third is thus not in Hegel, as many superficial readers of Hegel suggest, the transcendental third party that from the outside unites the two which are equally transcendentally lying outside each other, opposing each other. The whole force of the dialectical cunning of Hegelian "speculative judgment" as opposed to formal judgment lies precisely here: that in being passing into non- being, and non-being passing into being (thus not remaining transcendental in relation to each other)[5], what remains non-passing is this *hama*, *simul* of the non-hama, of non-simul. Since *hama* presents itself even in its negativity as immanent, the negativity (the non-being of death) therefore converts itself into being. This is the secret power of death, death's work—this ability to *contract*, *gather* into Now, into the being of Now, the nows of the non-beings: the non-being of the already having been, the non-being of the yet-to-be, and the being that is passing into non-being. Note that these nows whose being consists in their non-being *are* only to the extent that they are in relation to *Now*, the eternal presence in every present, in every now. In every now, in every non-being, Now presents itself as *hama*. There are non-beings because there *are* these non-beings; in other words, their *being* consists of being non-beings and that is what Hegel thinks of in terms of *hama*. There are nows only because Now presents itself in every now; they are merely variations of the Now, which Hegel also calls "eternity". Therefore, presence Now and eternity, although seemingly irreconcilable opposites to a common-sense way of thinking, are not so from a dialectical standpoint: they are one and the same, for only presence can be eternity and eternity be presence. Eternity is *contraction*, gathering, in the sense of *hama*, of nows: this is simultaneously present in non-beings of that which has been and that which is not yet. Therefore, in Hegel's *Philosophy of Nature* (1970), time *appears* as the negation of space (time that negates itself as having to appear)—since it cannot maintain itself in its sheer unrest of negativity—and thus passes into space. This space is not the space of the already negated, and yet the same, dialectically understood, as that which subsumes its difference within itself, that is, the space which is *Now*: this is gathering of the dispersed into the self-same and contraction of the multiplicity of various nows into the simultaneity of the eternal Now.

Having said this, the question now becomes more acute: if messianic has something to do with the here and now, can this now (the messianic now) be thought of as the same Now as *contraction*, i.e. as *hama* or *simul*? When one says (whether it is Derrida or Rosenzweig) that messianic is *at the same time, at once* the "here and now" and "coming" (of the future), is this "same time" the same as *hama*—for *hama* means *simul* (simultaneity)? If not, then this same time is not the same time of *contraction* either. There may happen a now—a here and now—which is not a contraction of nows, whose plenitude or fulfilment does not arrive through a contraction of nows, but in a now outside this process and outside the labour of contraction, outside the work of *hama*: a messianic *coming* here and now.

If messianic arrives here and now, what does it mean to say that messianic is the affirmation of the yet to arrive, since what is yet to arrive must exceed, must be otherwise than a "here and now"? For is it not that two presents cannot exist together? Two nows cannot coexist, for the moment one now arrives, it negates by a necessary logic the other now, so that there can only be a now if, or when, other nows become non-nows at the same time. If there is messianic arriving now, so the question persists, it cannot be at the same time another now (since two nows cannot co-exist). One may, however, respond to this supposed contradiction of the messianic time in this way: if one says that coming now is another now, different from "here and now", and that there can therefore be messianic arriving here and now at this "here and now" and also this messianic coming of "here and now" in another "here and now" that is in the future of "here and now", then there is no contradiction here at all of messianic time, for one may affirm both *heres* and *nows* at the same time. There is a here and now of messianic *coming* at the present of the "here and now", and there will also be a messianic here and now in the coming future, which is also a coming here and now. What prohibits one from affirming both?

However, this response is immediately met with scepticism. If one says that nothing prohibits one from affirming both a "here and now" at one time and another "here and now" at another time, they are not affirmed at the same time, but affirmed at different times. Therefore, one cannot affirm at the same time both a messianic time of the here and now, of presence, and a messianic time of the future. Either of the two holds true: either one says that the messianic time arrives here and now, which is presence, or that messianic time is still *to* come, is awaited and hoped for in a future that has not yet arrived. They cannot be affirmed at the same time absolutely and unconditionally as the same time, but *they can both be affirmed at different times*, since both are not present at the same time.

The question is simply this: how can two times (or many times) be affirmed at the same time if each time cancels the other out, if they are incommensurable with each other such that no reconciliation or sublation occurs? For different times can be affirmed at the same time only if there is contraction, or *hama*. The latter is the dialectical resolution. To affirm different times at the same time that would have no characteristic of sublation has to happen in a time which is impossibility of time itself, impossibility of time to present itself to itself, the impossibility of any unity of self-presence and the impossibility of the self-presentation of time. The messianic arriving is the impossibility of this self-presentation of time. The messianic does not arrive *in* time—neither *in* the here and now, nor *in* the future. It is the impossibility of experiencing time, an impossibility of time of experiencing, either as/in the here and now or as/in the coming future. Yet the messianic arrives, or comes as ecstatic-ahead-of-itself: this arriving is not a particular mode of time, which is future that will come to pass. It is that which arrives as ever-remaining arriving, which will not come to pass as mere mode of presence. How can this be understood?

When one asks: how can one say that messianic arrives here and now and, at the same time, say that it is still *coming*?—as if there is a contradiction—what notion of time is presupposed? Is it not the same Hegelian view of time that is tacitly presupposed, that there cannot be many nows together, that one may not affirm two nows at the same now, that if they have to be affirmed together, they must be affirmed with the Hegelian affirmation as *hama*, which does not seem to be what is affirmed in messianic coming, for there is nothing really to come in the Hegelian process, for each now generates its own negation, and negation negates its own negativity? Messianic *coming* of the other is something other than the *auto-production*, or *autochthony* of temporality, for this auto-production of temporality cannot be thought of other than as negativity, for *only as negativity may time produce itself and close itself in its circular reappropriation.* Thus, what notion of time is presupposed when one says that someone cannot say without contradiction that messianic arrives here and now and, at the same time, is still coming?: what is presupposed here are two particular times—of here and now, and coming future—which means a *particularity* of temporalities, which tacitly allows one to think that messianic arrives *in* time. Then, the messianic arriving is already levelled off to the "homogenous empty time" that Benjamin (1977: 258) speaks of, for the particularity of temporalities can be subsumed under what Hegel calls "Being in General" (1998: 60), the universal order of time, determined by the Concept and arrested, contracted and subsumed under the dialectical *hama*, the synchronic modality of onto-theo-logic. The ecstatic of singular temporalities is heard no more, but each of the ecstatic transcendences is levelled off to the "they". Therefore the notion of messianic coming is intimately tied up with transcendence. There is no messianic arrival if there is no transcendence, and no ecstatic outside, above and beyond the given. It is this beyond, this thinking of the outside, this thinking of transcendence and ecstatic, that is the essence of messianic: it is not the future as the particular mode of a homogenous, empty scale of time. If the thinking of transcendence, the beyond and outside is also a future, this future is not the future of the specific temporality: there are singular ecstatic temporalities only to the extent that each one, in its singular way, is *attuned* to coming, each one is ahead of itself, and there lie the ecstasies of each one of them. Here, it is necessary to elaborate the notion of *attunement* of coming time as transcendence, which can be understood as follows: there is ecstatic past, ecstatic present and the ecstatic future only because each one of them is *attuned* to the ecstatic ahead-of-itself, exceeds itself, transcends itself; there is no ecstatic past, ecstatic present or ecstatic future without each one being *attuned* to the transcendence of itself. This *aheadness*, this forward dimension, this opening to the *coming*, is the originary of finite existence: "this" futurity, which is not a future as one of the three dimensions of time, is messianic future, a futurity and coming other than "future". This futurity does not therefore arrive, or come *in* time, let alone some future time: what comes as coming, this messianic coming, is not this or that coming, but *coming itself*. Coming comes: messianic coming. Messianic comes. Messianic comes here and now. But the messianic does not come *in* the here and now, in a self-present, self-contained temporality of plenitude and fulfilment; its fulfilment is of transcendence, overflowing, bursting and giving birth, redemption in the ever-coming. It is because this coming comes in each of the ecstatic temporalities that there comes coming "here and now". There comes coming past; there comes coming present; there comes coming future: each one of the ecstasies is its futurity—the ecstatic past is its futurity; the ecstatic present is its futurity; the ecstatic future is also its futurity. Each one leaps ahead of itself, and opens to the arriving.

The future of messianic is the ever coming that comes. Therefore Rosenzweig, in *The Star of Redemption* (2005), calls it the "everlasting kingdom of the coming" that remains *coming*. It is from here that the notion of *remaining* is elaborated: the time that *remains*. For there to remain remaining, for time *to* remain, means to have time beyond death, time to remain after all ends of time, time to remain after every last time, after all last time. Rosenzweig calls it "redemption". It is coming that redeems historical time, and also redeems death, for the metaphysics of history is the work of death, an *anamnesis* of *what has been* by passing through. Remember what Hegel beautifully evokes at the end of his *Phenomenology of Spirit*, where the intimate relationship between speculative phenomenology and history is articulated—the "gallery of images" (Hegel 1998: 492–493)? Messianic coming must point towards the outside of this metaphysics of death, which means the *thetic* time of the historical, for *death does not redeem time, but is coming time, remaining ever, which redeems death.*

This is what should not be ignored when one thinks of messianic time: that the messianic time is thinking of redemption on the basis of the remaining time, and not on the basis of death; that it is death that must be thought of on the basis of time, and not time on the basis of death. If there remains the remaining time, it is because in the arrived—which means that which is accomplished, finished and thetic, that which has become stale and dead—there remains something yet to come. This non-arrived in all that has arrived points forward to the *coming* that remains beyond all that is finished, all that is dead and death. It is therefore not annihilation or destruction of time, or even death of time, rather it is what remains to arrive as everlasting arriving redemption, beyond death. It remains to arrive here and now, therefore one says that there is a yet to come here and now. There is futurity here and now, there comes coming here and now, and without this coming and remaining, there is neither past, present nor future.

It is therefore not a question, or the problem, of the necessity and impossibility of affirming two different *particular* times at the same time. We must now reformulate the problem. It is precisely because there comes coming that we affirm here and now. There is no necessity, or demand, to affirm here and now if coming does not come, if a here and now does not remain that has not yet arrived. The here and now is not one of the particular dimensions of temporalities of one universal time—namely the present—but remaining time itself. Rosenzweig calls it "ever-renewed birth of the soul" (Rosenzweig 2005: 169). Because the eternal past remains eternally the past, it remains eternally past here and now, in ever- renewed presence, and also remains eternally past in the future that is not yet redeemed. This is the thought of the messianic. It is not the time of particular future that will happen sometime, but this thinking of the remains. This question of messianic can be illuminated only if this problem of time is clarified.

The ages of the world

Schelling's *The Ages of the World* (2000) struggles with this question: how does one think of different times at the same time (*Zusammenhang*), which does not have the character of thetic, which means that it would not have the nature of *hama*? This demands the deconstruction of the dominant metaphysics of judgment, and the notion of the copula that this metaphysics of judgment determines it to be, in so far as this notion of judgement is essentially predicative. The predicative proposition, so far as it thinks of copula as thetic *hama*—and thus merely as *anamnesis* of a speculative phenomenology—does not think of being as coming, in its genesis, in its *apophantic* coming to be. Therefore deconstruction of the dominant metaphysical notion of judgment—and all that it entails, namely the identity principle that the traditional notion of copula suggests, the *thetic* nature of *hama* which is the copula, etc.—is tied to the question of coming: how one thinks of *coming* that is not the coming of this or that, but this *coming* itself. It would be necessary for one to undertake, in a deconstructive gesture, to articulate the complex relationship between the metaphysics of temporality as presence and the metaphysical foundation of logic wherein privilege is accorded to the predicative proposition. Schelling's works, from *Human Freedom* (1992), through *The Ages of the World* (2000), to his last Berlin lectures on mythology (2007) and revelation (1977), therefore attempt to think of human freedom and the ecstatic existentiality of existence in its very *coming to presence* which demands deconstruction of the metaphysics of judgment and presence. Here, Schelling grasps the hidden foundation and ground of the possibility of this metaphysics: the intimate and innermost connection between language and time, between judgement and the thetic reduction of the ecstatic genesis, the reduction of the *apophantic* dimension of judgment to the predicative proposition. He thereby shows that the possibility of this metaphysics, even when such a metaphysics of judgement undertakes to think of the notion of judgement as merely negative, as negative judgement, lies in its inability to think of existence and coming other than as *thetic* and as *hama*. Schelling, however, without renouncing the question of judgement altogether, attempts to think otherwise than in relation to *hama* and to the thetic, which means as otherwise than dialectical negativity, without sublation, without *Aufhebung*. This demands the rigor of a thinking, at its limit a thinking that ventures beyond even philosophy, of an abysmal non-oppositional duality whose resolution of the tension would not have the character of the *hama*, which would not have *Aufhebung* as the very possibility of a philosophical system, for it is no longer the dialectical opposition of concepts, but *real* oppositions in its *actuality*, for conceptual oppositions are only *possible* oppositions and not the actual. In order to think not merely of possible oppositions, one must venture beyond the negative philosophy, and thus even beyond a conceptual system. Thus, instead of thinking in terms of categories whose oppositions are merely possible oppositions, Schelling asks us to think of the real opposition that existence, in its very coming, has to a ground outside it, to the groundless, to the abyss that refuses to be articulated in the predicative proposition—that existence expels, excludes or lifts itself, as it were, above its ground (but not as *Aufhebung*) in order to come *to* existence, or in order to come *to* presence. In order to come *to* presence, this *coming* excludes its very ground of coming to be, for the ground itself excludes itself and is thus *Abgrund*, the abyss, the unground, the non-condition. Thus, each coming *to* presence posits its ground as past (the "that-has-been", or, the ground) which is a *not-having-being* and therefore is the eternal past; it is the ground that eternally *remains* in eternal coming to be as an eternal *remnant*.

The question of the *remains*, or *remnant*, can be articulated as this question of beginning and the question of ground (and not as the question of the end result of the process that has dialectically accumulated its presents), for only when thinking seriously confronts the enigma of the beginning is the *coming* in its existentiality—irreducible to any predicative thinking—confronted and addressed. Here is the sharpest distinction between this manner of thinking and the dialectical process of historicity, for the *predicative* process of this history does not address this *coming* as the very question of beginning, for it does not confront the coming, for which the thinking of coming is none other than anamnesis, a tracing back.

In *The Ages of the World* (2000), Schelling thinks of this question of the beginning as follows: because there remains the ground as ground, the past remains as eternal past—and therefore the eternal remnant of the past as past (and not as presence), the abyss itself—and in each coming to presence there remains the past as the remainder. There cannot be a coming if there is none of the remaining, but this remaining, since it is the un-prethinkable decision, the cision[6], this cision as the very condition of coming, or beginning of existence, falls outside the junction that joins, while separating, the ground and existence as the very condition of their relation. Therefore this *cision*, this *cut*, the abysmal copula, does not function as *hama* as in a predicative proposition, as in the metaphysics of judgement; it does not sublate as the thetic negativity does, for it does not contract in self-presence in any present the disjunction of ground and existence, the disjunction of the eternal past and the eternal coming, for it is precisely this disjoining which makes possible "the same time" of the eternal past remaining with, which means without, the eternal here and now. What holds together (*Zusammenhang*) does not belong to the jointure, to the system of the judgement: it remains the excluded wound, so that the cision or the cut may call towards each other in their very separation. The eternal past as eternal past is not thereby pure nothing, nor is it "this" something, but in its "not-having-being", which means it *remaining* not-having-being—which is not pure nothing, and therefore its "not having being" is not determined as lack of determination (for Hegel, nothing, as speculatively opposite to being, means lack of determination)—it is to cut *away*, so that a cut *towards* happens, so that there comes the coming. This is the birth of time, the apophantic origination of time, as the cision of ground and existence—born out of the un-prethinkable *de-cision*—the inauguration of coming. Without this cutting away, hence cutting towards—without this *cutting*, this *de-cision* and *cision*—there is thus neither coming nor that anything that is posited as past: it falls outside, therefore in a certain sense is prior to beginning, as the un-prethinkable, irreducible to the predicative (for the predicative is derived from the originary apophantic cision, that there must already be the beginning, or birth, of existence outside predication so that there be predication), before the concept and before historical-speculative time—a beginning before beginning that remains as beginning and does not lapse into nothing. The beginning before any beginning—and thus *lengthening, stretching* of time beyond any dialectical historical closure—does not cease to begin in each coming, in eternal future and eternal presence. Since it remains as eternally beginning, it remains only as past, a never-passed past: that is how different times co-exist at the same time, a co-existence understood as cision of the remnant. There comes coming because, in a certain sense, it has already come. Therefore, a certain saying goes that the Messiah who is yet to come has come already. This means that the messianic has not ceased coming, but is the eternally coming other: there is no here and now where coming may not come, and no here and now where the other may not arrive. This coming is the breathing of time: the plenitude of the here and now, this moment, this presence, without delay and without procrastination. This *coming* eternally coming is also thereby the eternal awaiting for the other who remains to come, whose coming has remained even when history is finished and accomplished, even when the labour of the negative is complete. This future, the eternal future of beginning, and the eternal beginning of future, does not belong to predicative knowledge, even to absolute knowledge of dialectical philosophy. The thinking of future is the limit of knowledge and limit of philosophical thinking.

The event of the outside

The *coming* attunes to the eternal past, which is the principle of beginning, the dark principle of the ground that remains, and remains the possible as the unceasing, ever-remaining condition. But this dark principle, the most primordial, is not the most important one, for there may come something other than mere creation, another coming beyond the darkness of the beginning and ground may be thought of, for "only on account of the future" is existence cheerful (Schelling 2000: 42). That existing one may reveal to himself what is created, there may be revelation and manifestation of coming *here and now*, thus this eternal presence, here and now, cannot be revealed if something is not posited as past so that the dark principle be transfigured into the principle of light. Only then does presence come into itself *here and now*, becomes itself, is now coming into itself, giving birth to itself, by relegating the eternal past to the darkness of the eternally possible ground; the revelation brings and transfigures the past to the light of the *here and now* because the eternal past is not sufficient in itself; as mere ground and mere possibility it is *yearning* for something other than itself. Hence, the coming of the *here and now* is born out of yearning for the otherwise. According to Schelling:

> There is no dawning of consciousness (and precisely for this reason no conscious- ness) without positing something past. There is no consciousness without some- thing that is at the same time excluded and contracted. That which is conscious excludes that of which it is conscious as not itself. Yet it must again attract it precisely as that of which it is conscious of itself, only in a different form. That which is consciousness is simultaneously the

> excluded and attracted can only be the unconscious. Hence all consciousness is grounded on the unconscious and precisely on the dawning of consciousness the unconscious is posited as the past of consciousness. (Schelling 2000: 44)

The eternal past remains eternally past in the ever-new *revelation* of the here and now, in ever-renewed here and now. However, this remnant of the eternal past, precisely because it remains *only* as eternal past and even though it is renewed ever anew in the eternally present of the here and now, in so far as it is renewal only in relation to that which is the eternally past, there precisely lies the need for redemption, which may arrive only in the coming time. Here, the notion of the messianic in relation to the coming has a decisive relation to future, which, again, is not understood as the particular instance of homogenous, empty measure of a linear, temporal scale. Rather, it is the distress and melancholy of the eternal past, the withdrawal abyss of the ground, and also the revelation of this estranged truth here and now of the eternal presence that renews the truth of the eternal past, and thus is always in relation to the eternal past. It is because the melancholy of the eternal past has remained unredeemed in any present now, this unredeemed past requires redemption. Therefore the everlasting relation that the messianic has with time in its true profundity is with a time wholly otherwise. The coming time of the messianic is not the future time as one particular dimension of time (where its now is homogenous with the other two nows). The latter gives us the (Hegelian) dialectical-speculative conception of Now as the eternal presence: such Now eternally will then be present in all nows homogenously. One should not here forget Benjamin's beautifully evoked "homogenous empty time" (Benjamin 1977: 258). Rather, the messianic coming, if its futurity be grasped in true profundity, is time wholly otherwise, the other time, or better, otherwise than time, for only a time wholly otherwise may redeem the eternal abyss of the past, the unspeakable melancholy of finite life and eternally revealed truth of that abyss. For that to be possible, time—a wholly otherwise time—must remain beyond past and beyond presence, even though that past is eternal and presence is eternal presence: this wholly otherwise time is the coming time beyond death which redeems this abyss of the past. This remaining may redeem the remainder of death, the remainder of the beginning and its eternally past abyss. This remaining of the coming is the thinking of redemption and therefore the thinking of redemption is always thinking of the future. If there is need of redemption, it is because the eternal death and the eternal abyss of the past require a *coming* time. This coming time may therefore have to *remain* after death. It is here that the complexity of the gesture of messianic thinking of Rosenzweig, already anticipated in Schelling's later works, is articulated with clarity. Both *The Star of Redemption* (Rosenzweig 2005) and *The Ages of the World* (Schelling 2000) begin with the question of eternal past, with death, and with eternal beginning; and towards the end of his book Rosenzweig points towards the urgency and the imminence of redemption that is *coming* which cannot be thought of on the basis of a speculative anamnesis, that cannot be articulated in the predicative process of history.

Redemption is the event that is the outside; it is the event of the outside. To be redeemed is to have time beyond and outside death—this is the meaning of a messianic remnant, of a messianic hope beyond despair. Hope redeems despair and is eternally open to the arriving of the other, the wholly otherwise. The primordiality of hope, and the primordiality of hope in relation to messianic time, does not lie, therefore, in tracing back to the abysmal dark ground of existence, nor merely in the renewal in the presence of what has arrived—for there always remains non-arrived in the arrived—but in the forward-looking for what has *not yet* arrived, and *yet* which must arrive "today", "here and now". Therefore the messianic arriving of here and now is not to be understood as that which arrives in a conditioned present (or historical present), where *something* has arrived or is arriving, but more essentially and primordially. It is the demand, the exigency of the messianic that if the coming does not come here and now, it does not come at all. This means that the wholly otherwise may come here and now, that the here and now may be wholly otherwise, that today "today" may be wholly otherwise than today. This imminent *coming* must remain even though any given present ("today", a historical present) has passed away so that the-today (a today wholly otherwise, the unconditional which is irreducible to the historical present) remains the here and now *of* coming. Today (in the historical, dialectical, conditioned present) there remains the excess of a today which is wholly otherwise (a today which is messianic, the unconditional coming); the latter today is here and now and yet wholly otherwise, therefore wholly future. The messianic future comes today, here and now.

Wholly otherwise

The difficulty of understanding the messianic time arises from our thinking of time in the traditional metaphysical way, where temporalities, in their three nows, are grasped as a linear succession. Therefore, despite Hegel's endeavours to think of time more primordially[7], the traditional determination of time retains its sovereignty. This is most visible when Hegel, in his *Philosophy of Nature* (1970), determines time in its negativity as sublated again to space (though time negates space in its indeterminacy so that the arrangement of various nows is accomplished in the modality of spatiality), even though it is succession that is at stake here. The messianic time—in its supposed contradiction of having to affirm both the here and now and the future of the coming—becomes incomprehensible when temporality is understood in the aforementioned manner. It is thus important to attend that the notion of messianic time interrogates the dialectical-historical closure of time which thinks of time in the traditional-metaphysical way.

The messianic time must affirm the *wholly otherwise* of here and now, today, a *future of here and now.* If it is not affirmed here and now—this wholly otherwise—then it is not affirmed ever. This imminence and urgency that brings together here and now, and the wholly otherwise is not dialectical-historical contraction; it is not the gathering of various homogenous nows in the dialectical-historical self-presence. What is present here and now is not the self-presence, but the wholly otherwise redeeming one that disjoins today *from* today, a here and now *from* here and now. The wholly otherwise comes as the *tearing* of time from itself, separation of itself from itself, cutting away (Schelling's *Scheidung*). As Schelling beautifully says that even God's giving birth to himself demands God's withdrawal, separation of himself from himself, disjoining and cutting away of himself from himself so that spacing opens, or better, there opens an opening, an opening to the un-prethinkable, incalculable and un-predicative coming: thus the otherwise than God himself comes *to* presence. This is God's un-prethinkable *de-cision*: this *apophantic* origination of time before any self-present "origin", this beginning of time before beginning, demands that God makes his own nature its eternal ground, which means the excluding of his own nature from his existence, so that he becomes what he is, the actually existing One. All coming, all births of the kingdom, all arrivals need this tearing, this disjoining, which means *spacing* or opening. Something must be posited as other than oneself, or something otherwise, a holly otherwise may be hoped for. Something must be posited as the past so that the wholly otherwise comes. Therefore Schelling says that someone who never posits something as past does not have future or presence. He does not have either birth or redemption.

NOTES

1. The relationship between the problem of the temporality of the future and the possible is extremely complex and difficult to deal with here. Both Ernst Bloch and Søren Kierkegaard—two thinkers of the future, although very different from each other—were profoundly influenced by Schelling's thinking from *The Ages of the*

World (2000) onwards. While in *The Ages of the World* Schelling introduces the notion of potencies through which he seeks to grasp the very *coming* of the historical world and time itself, through cision and rupture, in his later lectures on the groundwork of positive philosophy Schelling attempts to open the regressive movement of the negative philosophy of Hegel to the progressive movement of positive philosophy, which consists of opening to the coming of future that cannot be reduced to the predicative thinking of negative philosophy. These lectures on positive philosophy, attended by Kierkegaard, left deep impressions in Kierkegaard's writings, especially in *The Concept of Anxiety* (2001). In *The Concept of Anxiety*, he thus makes a connection between three notions: the category of the *possible* (irreducible to the actualized and realized), the temporality of the *future* and the mood of *anxiety*. Thus, Kierkegaard (or Vigilius Haufniensis) writes: 'The possible corresponds exactly to the future. For freedom, the possible is the future, and the future is for time the possible. To both of these corresponds anxiety in the individual life. An accurate and correct linguistic usage therefore associates anxiety and the future' (2001: 201). The possible, for Kierkegaard, is irreducible to the realized and the actual, for while the actual is only a limitation of the possible and therefore finite, the possible is infinite and calls forth faith, since faith demands education in the possible: 'Whoever is educated by anxiety is educated by possibility, and only he who is educated by possibility is educated according to his infinitude. Therefore possibility is the weightiest of all categories' (2001: 203). For Ernst Bloch, too—whom Habermas called 'Marxist Schelling'—possibility is one of the most important notions, which he, in a manner different from Kierkegaard, also connects with the anticipatory thinking of the future and thereby affirms the thinking of a messianic utopia.

2. Thus Kierkegaard writes: 'In possibility all things are equally possible, and whoever has truly been brought up by possibility has grasped the terrible as well as joyful' (2001: 203).
3. It is here that the cryptic remark Schelling makes towards the end of his *Philosophical Inquiries into the Nature of Human Freedom* becomes illuminating: that even in God, there must have been a sadness,

which becomes unappeasable in mortals, because for creation to be possible, an opening to the possible, to something other than God himself is required of God; and yet this melancholy in God, in whom it never attains actuality but remains a mere possibility, this alone affirms the necessity of yet to come, the necessity of a joyous labor of creation. (see Schelling 1992: 79). This means none other than that our ethico-political task of creation, which requires an opening towards the outside, towards the possible and the wholly otherwise, towards a coming of a redemptive future, is attuned to a melancholy, and also thereby an affirmation of hope in the coming, for the creative task of mortals demands that 'joy must have sorrow and sorrow must be transfigured in joy' (Schelling 1992: 79).

4. If there are two equal beings, or if there are two equal non-beings, then there is no dialectical opposition. On the other hand, if there is always unequal, incommensurable contradiction between a non-being and a being, then there is no dialectic either, for that would be 'bad infinity'. This contra- diction, this aporia, can be resolved only if there is identity between the identity of the non-being and the being on the one hand, and difference between the non-being and the being on the other.
5. Here we have Hegel's famous critique of Kant.
6. Cision means 'cut', 'slit', 'separation', 'disjunction' or 'divorce'. *Scheidung* means 'de-cision', and also 'cision' or 'cut'. In addition, *Scheidung* means 'vagina', the opening of the female genitalia that is also a separation or cut, the slit of two lips that opens. *Scheidung* has the connotation of opening, or coming, which is at once separation and disjunction.
7. Than Kant (for example): this means Hegel's attempt to think of time not merely formally but as the very coming and passing (things do not come in time, so Hegel argues, but things which come themselves are coming and passing away).

REFERENCES

Benjamin, Walter, 'Über den Begriff der Geschichte' in *Illuminationen* (Frankfurt: Suhrkamp, 1977), pp. 251–261.

Bloch, Ernst, *The Principle of Hope,* Vol. 1, trans. N. Plaice, S. Plaice and P. Knight (Cambridge, MA: The MIT Press, 1986).

Derrida, Jacques, 'Ousia and *Gramme*: Note on a Note from *Being and Time*', in *Margins of Philosophy,* trans. Alan Bass (Chicago: University of Chicago Press, 1982), pp. 29–68.

Hegel, G.W.F., *Philosophy of Nature,* trans. A.V. Miller (Oxford: Clarendon Press, 1970).

Hegel, G.W.F., *Phenomenology of Spirit,* trans. A.V. Miller (Delhi: Motilal Benarasidass, 1998).

Heidegger, Martin, *Hölderlins Hymnen 'Germanien' und 'Der Rhein* (Frankfurt: Vittorio Kloster mann, 1980).

Kierkegaard, Søren, 'The Concept of Anxiety' in *The Kierkegaard Reader,* eds. J. Chamberlain and J. Rée (Oxford: Blackwell, 2001), pp. 180–210.

Rosenzweig, Franz, *The Star of Redemption,* trans. Barbara E. Galli (Madison: The University of Wisconsin Press, 2005).

Schelling, F.W.J. von, *Philosophie der Offenbarung* (Frankfurt am Main: Suhrkamp, 1977).

Schelling, F.W.J. von, *Philosophical Inquiries into the Nature of Human Freedom,* trans. J. Gutmann (La Salle, Illinois: Open Court, 1992).

Schelling, F.W.J. von, *The Ages of the World,* trans. Jason Wirth (Albany, New York: State University of New York Press, 2000).

Schelling, F.W.J. von, *Historical-Critical Introduction to the Philosophy of Mythology,* trans. M. Richey (Albany, New York: State University of New York Press, 2007).

Of force, of rhythm, of melody

> I fear we are not getting rid of God because we still believe in grammar...!
>
> —Friedrich Nietzsche (1968: 38).

On the metaphysical foundation of grammar

For a long time, perhaps always, mankind has cherished the most ancient metaphysical dream, namely this: to be able to discover, or construct the foundational structure of human community or thought in the name of Being or meaning (they amount to the same: the meaning of Being and the Being of meaning) that itself would be beyond the contingency of human experience, beyond the manifoldness of its ceaseless coming and going in the flow of time that would not abide by. As such, human experience—perhaps I should rather say 'human existence'—has been a source of grief for philosophers or metaphysicians: human existence, with its enigmatic finitude seems to elude the grasp of human 'reason' and all the claims that reason is called upon to evoke. In other words, what has been a source of both dream and grief for the metaphysician is nothing but this: dream of the grammar that must be able to provide for mankind the foundational ontological structure that itself would not come to pass but whose essence is graspable in the light of theoretical comprehension. From Plato to Hegel via Leibniz's 'universal characteristics'—perhaps we must include Heidegger too—this theoretical light illumines our dream. Twentieth century's linguistic study that seeks to constitute itself as science is only the utmost assertion of this metaphysical dream of grammar. One often is oblivious of the metaphysical foundation of this grammar, that it is nothing but our most ancient metaphysical need wherein lies our most unseen evaluation, our assertion or negation of forces that would be evaluated according to our need. Thus the question would no longer be Kantian: How grammar is possible (as Kant asks, how *a priori* synthetic judgment is possible?) but rather, whether it is at all desirable to have grammar, or perhaps even better, (to ask with Nietzsche) what kind of forces are there according to what need that evaluate or desire this grammar as the fundamental structure of language itself. Why grammar is a necessity for a certain force so that beneath the whispers and silences between words, beneath the gestures and tonal fluctuations of saying one would seek to discover/recover the absolute formal structure which would account for those fluctuations and whispers once and for all? The grammarians and the linguists are those theoreticians and metaphysicians for whom grammar is only a displacement of God when God has disappeared—perhaps only to appear as the grammarian! Or perhaps, it is better to say that God has been conceived by mankind as the first, and hence the most perfect (since "origin" is what constitutes the most perfect) grammarian par-excellence: someone who says for the first time, "let there be light" or someone, who being the primordial Being, utters the most primordial word—the word beyond all words, silence beyond all silences. That God must be the first speaker, that there must have been the first speaker from which all speech originates: this metaphysical presupposition is the origin of the desire to constitute the meta-language as grammar.

What holds sway all throughout, however, is the primacy of the theoretical: grammar is theoretical knowledge par-excellence.

What is important for us to consider that the notion of 'Science' itself is inextricably linked to the metaphysical determination of the theoretical: theoretical apprehension of the thing-in-itself is what constitutes *logos*, saying or speech. Hence, the onto-logical determination of language itself is grammar. Thus grammatical-speculative[1] is inseparably bound up with the question of Being and the manifold meanings of Being: the theory of meaning or form is essentially a question of Being and vice versa[2]. Let us pursue this question little further. If the metaphysical determination of the identity of Being and saying (its language) realizes itself in the onto-theo-logical determination of the Subject in its historicity, then language itself becomes history. This is what happens with Hegel's onto-theo-logical constitution of metaphysics. When, long after Plato's meditations on language and Aristotle's thought on language, language again becomes the problematic site in the late eighteenth and early nineteenth century, for example from Herder to Hegel, the old metaphysical desire for grammar assumes the form of historicity. Therefore it is not surprising that for Hegel history itself becomes 'science'. It is here, however, we must be aware that for Hegel 'science' means very different thing than what we mean nowadays (for example, by linguistics as science). Granted that, what persists and what goes unquestioned. however, in Hegelian onto-theo-logical determination of the historicity of Being as Subject and in our present-day linguist's dream of constituting language itself as science is this: the primacy of the theoretical that must be able to provide the fundamental structure of human thought or human language, a kind of grammar that is apprehensible through scientific knowledge. Whether this grammar is conceived in the form of a phenomenological-historical narrative for the absolute Spirit that effectuates itself as 'negativity' (for Hegel, language is this negativity, the passage that negates the sensible to sublate it to the ideality of signification). This process, as we know, is called *Aufhebung*: as a historical-formal structure, language has always been conceived in the name of the ideality of presence or meaning that must be able to persist and thereby would recover and recuperate the foundational, underlying ontological form. Grammar is nothing but this ideality of linguistic structure, the ontological form of presence—abiding, persisting, subsisting and simultaneous with all that is non-simultaneity and non-contemporary: this grammar is seen as the condition of possibility of all human truth and knowledge. One might wonder whether this absolute structure—with Hegel this structure assumes the form of movement—is not at once arbitrary, and is itself a figurative or fictional construct, a discursive constitution, and thereby would not abide amidst what does not abide, if such a structure would not seek to be a mere fetish (which it would not seek to be): such a grammar, as pure saying, would say nothing of human experience but only murmur ceaselessly its emptiness, its own disappearance.

One must be able to go through the entire history of the metaphysical determination of language that would be able to show how the present-day linguist's desire to constitute meta-language itself has already been decided long back metaphysically[3], that this desire itself only a response to the metaphysical presuppositions which often go unnoticed, and unquestioned; and that these presuppositions themselves have their own history that dates long back. Not only how these structures (tree structure, for example) themselves have come into being, but also that this desire to constitute these supposedly timeless structures is only response to some far more profounder metaphysical need for evaluation (we will come to Nietzsche soon) which itself does not have any onto-logical structure graspable to theoretical vision, and that this response is only an assertion of certain will to power. The Hegelian desire to constitute the monumental system, as science, is this desire for grammar through which certain will to power asserts itself, a certain force asserts itself. There is, perhaps, no language-in itself (as there is no-thing-in itself); in other words, there is no Being of language, nor language of Being that would have grammatical structure for an onto-logy; rather, language is nothing but force affirming and negating itself in relation to other forces in their non-symmetrical differentiality, force affirming its will to power in its differential relation to other forces. Forces affirm language in its rhythm and melody: in other words, rhythm and melody are what forces affirm when they affirm themselves. Language is expression of this affirmation, which means this: there is neither one language nor is there any fundamental structure of language; but each time a force affirms, a singular meta-language asserts itself as sovereign *hegemonikon*; and since there is no the force but forces in their differential multiplicity, language itself is differential each time according to the forces that affirm themselves. The singular character of this 'each time' is because of the singularity of the rhythm and cadence: rhythm and cadence is singular each time and all the time. How this is to be understood?

Of force, of rhythm, of melody

> Socrates, practice music!
>
> —Nietzsche, citing Plato (Nietzsche 1967: 93)

What is important for us to emphasis here, with the help of Nietzsche, an entirely different view of language: language as force, the unconsciousness of language; or, to put it in another way, force as the unconsciousness of language. With this, one can see what at stake lies here, namely this: when at the beginning of nineteenth century, with Hegel followed by Herder, language is determined on the model of consciousness inasmuch as consciousness is already metaphysically determined as ideality of presence or as grammar (therefore it is not surprising that grammar has this inextricable relationship with consciousness. One only has to refer to, what came to be known in twentieth century as Cartesian Linguistics. Grammar is only reification or hypo-statization of consciousness as it has come to be metaphysically determined. All that is, however, well known), towards the end of nineteenth century, Nietzsche sought to emphasize that consciousness has its origin in far more profound unconscious willing and drive that itself would not have the ontological structure of meaning or concept, that itself is irreducible to the onto-logical structure. Which means this: that grammar of consciousness is only the reduced, constricted and petrified version of the far more subtle play of the differential multiplicity of unconscious forces, and that this unconsciousness of forces is manifested in the rhythmic and melodic way. Only by forgetting and petrifying the rhythmic and melody of language, the concept comes into being that leaves behind as remnant the ecstatic rhythm and melody. But the repressed character of language bursts forth in music and all works of art: force is this bursting forth, the rupturing of language. Melody and rhythm would then be thought as manifestation of unconscious forces that tear apart the being of language: behind the mask of Apollo, Dionysus bursts forth, the dismembering god. With this, something far more subtle and invisible takes place: the whole tradition of metaphysics itself is put into question. The whole tradition of metaphysics is seen to be the constriction and petrification of the differential multiplicity of the unconscious forces, of the rhythmic and melodic ecstasy through which forces manifest their will to power, evaluate other forces according to their need. What the grammarians lack is a sense of these unconscious forces of language and value of this sense; in other words, grammarians' lack of sense itself is evaluation, a response to a metaphysical need, itself only certain will to power. Therefore the task for us is no longer to construct grammar on the modality of the facts of consciousness, nor is it to make linguistics as science but to determine the sense and value of this will to power, or to determine and revaluate the unconscious forces, and to transform these forces into something affirmative. But this is what philologists and grammarians are incapable of doing. Hence is Nietzsche's refusal to remain a philologist. What does it mean to determine the value and sense of the will to power that is manifested as the forces express themselves through rhythm and melody? It is no longer to discover beneath the contingency of utterances the deep, inner grammatical structure but that the affirmative forces must assume—with rhythm and melody—the task of a critique. The task of the critique would not amount to be asking: what is the condition of possibility of a certain *a priori* principle, or structure or form which would be foundational and universal?; but rather this: the critique must assume for its task the valuation of forces, to determine how under certain condition, certain force has been able to affirm itself, and then also to be able to determine which force, among forces, needs to be affirmed, and how to create those conditions under which the force, which needs to be affirmed, can be affirmed. This means that it is a question of *valuation* (to determine which force is affirmative and which is not) and *interpretation* (the problematic of sense) and to determine the relation between the two—of valuation and interpretation. This is inseparable from two other problematic—*selection* and *breeding*—certain force would be selected and to be bred; but this *selection* and *breeding* already presupposes *valuation* and *interpretation*. In other words, it implies that certain discursive or linguistic force—since force is discursive—needs to be selected over others and must be bred. The question of politics is implied here. The question now becomes: why and in the name of what certain discourse would be selected? Would not it also amount to certain form of domination, or hegemony over others? Would it not thereby legitimize certain force affirming its will to power since all forces do not carry equal value? And more pressingly: from where that and in the name which that a certain force is given more value than others? To put the question more like Nietzsche: from where the very value of values itself does derive from? It is to this question that one must turn towards: the task of the critique is essentially political and the political is essentially critical. It is, however, important to emphasize the sense of the political implied here. For a long time, perhaps from Plato onward—I need only to refer to Plato's *Republic*—"political" has been given the sense of determining the ontological, fundamental structure of human community, or, of our social existence wherein language has been seen as transparent medium, in other word, representational. With this determination of the "political" and language as representational, metaphysics inaugurates its possibility. I mean by this: metaphysics is a particular determination of the "political" and of language as representation. The metaphysician is the theoretical individual par-excellence who determines the political and language in theoretical-metaphysical manner. Thus not only language is reduced to the grammatical but even the "political" has already been, surreptitiously, determined on the dialectic paradigm of the grammatical; or, should we say, the dialectical is nothing else but grammatical. The dialectician assumes the role of the grammarian: the political is reduced, in this way, to the determination of the grammatical structure of the human community, and language is seen as mere articulation of this grammar, or perhaps, itself is this grammar and nothing besides. Therefore one might say that language does not appear when grammar is seen to be the sovereign modal of thought, meaning or knowledge; or one might, for the same reason equally say that political does not appear when the political is reduced to the ontological-dialectical determination of human community. From Plato to Hegel the sovereignty of grammar and sovereignty of the dialectical-ontological modality of the "political" is not questioned. What rather happens from Plato to Hegel (via Descartes) is that of increasing interiorization and immanentization of the Platonic transcendental paradigm. Thus the "political" becomes the question of "consciousness" or "subject" rather than a transcendental "Being" or "Substance"; language becomes effectuating this "consciousness" or this "subject". What is remained unquestioned, even in Hegel, is the metaphysical presuppositions concerning this determination of the "political" (in relation to "subject" or "consciousness"), and this determination of language as representation of the above- mentioned sense of the "political". In either case, the political or language as such does not appear but made to serve the sovereignty of the theoretical, of the mastery of the grammar or of the "absolute negativity" (see Hegel's determination of the subject as "absolute negativity" in *Phenomenology of Spirit*) of the speculative subject. Or, should we put it in a grander manner: that human existence itself is not thought when there is God. Thus when we said—with Nietzsche as example—that critique is *political*, this *political* is to be understood as different from the dialectical-ontological-grammatical determination of human community. It is rather to differentiate from the metaphysical thought of "political": this is the task to make political itself appear, and language itself *to* appear. But that appears only when grammatical-ontological-dialectical determination of community or of language itself is put into question. This means that for the political and language to appear, political or language itself has to be critical and critical itself has to be political and linguistic. The task of the political is no longer to construct either a transcendental or immanent grammatical paradigm of the community, but rather to make itself appear as such at the *limit* of representation, at the infinite crisis of grammar and that—and this is important for us to emphasize—this crisis or limit has to be infinite. The political can only be infinite, and is nothing but this infinity (therefore there cannot be the end of History, in popular sense of the term, as it has become popular in recent days. There is, of course, end of History in a very different sense of the term: the endless end of History, the end that will never end having already ended, the end that is a task and not an occurrence) of the limit, the limit that cannot be subsumed to the negativity of the immanent Being-there-then as *Aufhebung* but that would exceed, in its infinity, any dialectical-grammatical-ontological politics of the "subject" or "consciousness". To put this problem simply is this: how to think the political and language without being reduced to the metaphysical determination of the "political", and to the grammatical determination of the language as representational so that political and language would appear (not as some essence manifesting its content in a phenomenological manner which can be grasped through eidetic or phenomenological reduction)? Perhaps there is no phenomenology of language or political appearing without being reduced to the representational structure of some essence. The task is rather to think the other way: that is to question how the relationship of language and the political can be thought (because language, in its non-contemporary relationship to itself, eludes the representational grasp of the dialectical-grammatical ontology, and furtively betrays this grasp while promising its fulfillment of pleasure)? How can, then, the relationship of the language and the political be thought inasmuch as political is not reduced the "politics"? This latter sense of "politics" is to be understood as the practical space of conditioned negotiations where juridico-strategic decisions of various kinds are made. It is here the question of force is introduced. What remained unthought in metaphysics that constitutes itself on the dialectical-grammatical-ontological paradigm of thought is this relationship of political and language as *force*. When it is said that forces are unconscious, it is to say that forces cannot be thought on the dialectical-grammatical paradigm of thought that takes "facts of consciousness" as the source and origin of thought. The thought of force here is thus a displacement of the metaphysical determination of "political" and language as representational. This new political cannot be based on the metaphysical politics of the subject, or on "consciousness", or, on ontological basis of philosophical grammar. Forces are the limit of representation of any presumed or assumed sovereignty of the "subject" or "consciousness"; they are the limit of grammar or of an onto-theo-logy. To think forces is to the think the limit. How to think the limit, which is neither representational nor grammatical, neither dialectical nor onto-logical? In other words, if the limit is to be thought other than Hegelian limit (because Hegel sought to realize the utmost possibility of metaphysics) the question is: how to think the limit other than negativity?

On the political question of the limit: music and the limit of representation

> I consider that if only a few hundred people of the next generation will have from music what I have from it, then I anticipate an entirely new culture! Everything that is left over and cannot be grasped in terms of musical relations does of course sometimes disgust and horrify me.
>
> —Friedrich Nietzsche (1969: 85)

One must be able to go through the entire texts of Nietzsche in relation to the history of metaphysics—since we take Nietzsche as our point of departure, for it is he who thought all these things together (the problem of forces and the political, language and the unconscious, on the political-cultural question of aesthetics in relation to the metaphysical determination of thought as Being, etc.). Such a task, however, cannot be undertaken here. I would rather be content to sketch, in a very preliminary manner, the questions that are at stake here: that for Nietzsche—for us too—the question of the political is essentially a question of culture. How to create the condition of the culture of affirmative forces?: this is the question that Nietzsche never stops asking, especially more so in his earlier works. Thus in his "On the Uses and Disadvantages of History for Life", culture is defined as the "unity of artistic style in all the expressions of the life of a people" (Nietzsche 1997: 79). What is important for us here to emphasize that for Nietzsche even at that time, when he was quite young, the meaning of the political is not to construct or recount the historical becoming of the "time" but to becomes *untimely*, which means: to seek the condition of possibility of an affirmative culture which is "unity of artistic styles", the one that exceeds the historical becoming of the time; in other words, culture that would exceed the dialectical reconstruction of the historical world. Here, as we have seen, culture is understood on the musical characteristics of melody or harmony of music: culture must be musical, because music has its untimely character; it is the unity of artistic styles.

The task of the political is to create the conditions under which music develops, which means, culture as improved *physis* thrives: this is the task of the political (that is not the construction of any dialectical-ontological-grammatical principle of becoming timely or historical). This means: that music out of which tragedy develops—this idea is explicitly present in *The Birth of Tragedy*—is irreducible to the metaphysical reduction of language as conceptual; it cannot be understood as the linguist's or the philologist' reduction of language to some *a priori*, transcendental, universal meta-language (that I call here as "grammar"). Till now politics is understood dialectically-grammatically; politics is understood as a task to construct the foundational-ontological structure of human community; but now, since God is dead, the task of the political is to make culture musical which is irreducible to the conceptual, or, to the grammatical-dialectical structure of community. This also means that what is conceptual (which dialectician unearths beneath the whispers and tremors of utterances) or grammatical structure is only the reduction of what is musical or metaphorical: concepts are the petrified, pale ghostly remainder, the last evaporating residue of what is vibrant, dynamic and originary language that self-enhances itself. As it is absurd to say that the musical or the metaphorical is derived from the conceptual, it is also absurd to found political on the basis is merely grammatical-dialectical-ontological paradigm of language. In his "On Music and Words", drawing the analogy from Plato's *Phaedrus*, Nietzsche says:

> What an undertaking it must be to write music for a poem, that is, to wish to illustrate a poem by means of music, in order to secure a conceptual language for music in this way. What an inverted world! An undertaking that strikes one as if a son desired to beget his father! Music can generate images that will always be mere schemata, as it were, examples of its real universal content. But how should the image, the representation, be capable of generating music? Not to speak of the notion that the concept or, as has been said, the "poetical idea" should be capable of doing this! (Nietzsche 1980: 109).

Thus, the task is to make Socrates or Hegel, who is the theoretical man, practice music. Why the theoretical-dialectical man must practice music? It is because the theoretical man banishes from language what is the originary, the most dynamic of language: that is, melody or music itself. The metaphysical determination of language reduces the musicality, the tonal fluctuation of language, the intensity of language that expresses itself through gestures, and reduces them to the petrified image of the concepts, because the intensity of gestures and melody is irreducible to any ontological schemata of the conceptual language. Only by constricting the melodic and intensity of gestures the sovereignty of concepts are constituted. The metaphysical determination from Plato to Hegel sought for its task to found the "political" on the basis of the concept. Therefore it is not surprising that for Hegel Absolute Spirit is understood as "infinite negativity" of the absolute Concept (the Concept of all concepts). Thus when Nietzsche understands as the task of the political is to create the conditions of culture as 'unity of artistic styles', at stake here is the displacement of the whole tradition of the Platonic metaphysics itself. The concept (or, the dialectical-conceptual language) is repression of the political, of culture; in other words, the concept is the repression of language itself: the intensity of the tonal fluctuations which is that of melody and the gesture of language is repressed when language is reduced to the negativity of the concept. Thus music has something to do with the unconscious forces of language, which are repressed; only by forgetting these unconscious forces of language—that are manifested in melody and gesture—the concept as consciousness is to be found. The metaphysical determination of the "subject" as "consciousness"—as it is found expression in Hegel—is the repression of the musical essence of language, its unconscious working and unworking through gestures and melody. Therefore there cannot be a concept of political or of music; but the concept must be delivered to the musical essence of language, "politics" must be delivered to the political: this is the political task of creating culture. Then political would no longer be understood as effectuating, producing the essence of the metaphysical subject through labour and its negativity but this: that negativity be delivered to its unworking, to its destruction and disaster. Hence Nietzsche's idea of *tragic culture* or community (Nietzsche 1967): only then language itself would appear and the political would make its appearance. Therefore the political task would be two-fold: saying *No* to reactive forces, to the negativity of dialectic-grammatical programming of the metaphysics on the one hand; and on the other, an affirmation of the forces that affirm life, and affirm language in its musical essence that has been repressed in the grammatical-dialectical construction of community. This is what from *The Birth of Tragedy* onwards Nietzsche would refer to as *the tragic*: the political task that would consist of devaluation of values that have become decadent; and transvaluation or transfiguration of values into something higher, into something affirmative. Only music or art transvalues or transfigures values: the politics that is thought on the basis of this transfiguration of values would no longer be politics of the concept, but that of music that aesthetically redeems and transforms values. The grammatical-dialectical paradigm of the conceptual language has become decadent in its reification or hypostatization of existing values. It can only show—this is the gregarious character of any philosophical system, or the grammarian' desire to construct the system of principles and rules (phonological-morphological-syntactic rules)—how certain already existing values (they do not even talk of values, rather rules or principle) have become necessity. When such system—conceptual or grammatical—becomes sovereign that only shows the necessity of already existing values, a particular species of mankind becomes nihilist and decadent: thus grammarians and system creators are nihilists and decadents. The task—which defines what it means to be political—is not to show the necessity of morphological-phonological-syntactic rules; it is not to display the necessity of the hypostatization of values; it is not to show historical necessity of the destinal Spirit's becoming. The political task is rather to transfigure values and to introduce play (rhythm and melody are the plays of language) into our political destiny. This task would require that forces—affirmative forces—must be affirmed and be allowed their play. In other words, affirmative forces must be granted their affirmation. But it is possible only inasmuch as all the foundational gestures of metaphysics (the dialectical-grammatical) that has hitherto guaranteed human meaning and a sense of stability and a home of metaphysical comfort are taken away. This is what we mean by the limit: the limit of representation, the limit of the given sense of the "political", etc. If we talk of force, of melody and rhythm and the political task, it is because music affirms the limit of language, affirmative forces affirm the limit of given values and transform the given values into something 'yet to come', and announce a birth to come. In its trembling rhythm the birth of the future announces itself.

One can sense here why birth has its essential relationship to rhythm (and not to concept) and therefore to music. One must be able to go through the entire texts of the metaphysics—to displace or deconstruct the privilege granted to concept in its relation to presence (to time)—thereby to show that it forgets and represses the maternal rhythm of birth itself, a relation to the 'yet to come'. That task—enormous—must be undertaken another time. I would be content here only to say this birth can only be rhythmic, irreducible to the theoretical apprehension through *retention* and *protention*[4] because the concept, in its indissoluble link with the hypostatization of presence, cannot think the 'yet to come' of birth. Rhythm is what eludes the theoretical-grammatical apprehension of the "subject". Rhythm: the beating of heart, the flow of blood, the enigma of birth. The political or politics of the future and of the 'yet to come' would consist of giving rhythm its beating, to give melody its resonance, to give affirmative forces its task to transfigure values. Forces beat, forces resonate, forces affirm through transfiguration: this is the meaning of the political as we would like to think. Language which is rhythmic, resonant and affirmative: this is what needs to be thought and not some dialectic-syntactic rules of grammar. Thus the political question for us to be: how to make language rhythmic like the maternal rhythm of heart-beating, to make language resonate that must be able to transfigure values and announce the 'yet to come' incessantly and interminably, for all the time to come, every time, here and now? How to give language its rhythm and melody, resonance and beating so that it can infinitely announce the future, future that would be infinite in such a way that the birth it announces must also be infinite? How to think that? How to make Socrates practice music? This is the task of thinking when we talk of crisis of grammar, of the limit of representation or of the death of God. This also implies that crisis of grammar, the limit of representation or the death of God—whatever we speak of it—can only be task and not merely some occurrences that can be named and represented by means of the concept. This task implies that we must infinitely bring grammar to its crisis, and push representation to its limit, and ceaselessly bring God to his own abandonment. This task implies that language must be pushed to the limit so that at the limit language beats, resonates and trembles: in other words, so that it becomes music. To practice music is to make another thought of community to appear—not based on the theoretical apprehension of the essence of the community but through the dissolution of the grammar, through dissolution of the metaphysics of the "subject" to open towards the other(s): this relation to the other(s) is, what Nietzsche calls *empathizing*. In *Dawn of the Day* Nietzsche says:

> It is music, however, more than anything else that shows us what past-masters we are in the rapid and subtle divination of feelings and sympathy: for even if music is only the imitation of an imitation of feelings, nevertheless, despite its distance and vagueness, it often enables us to participate in those feelings, so that we become sad without any reason for feeling so, like the fools that we are merely because we hear certain sounds and rhythms that somehow or other remind us of the intonation

and the movements, or perhaps even only of the behavior, of sorrowful people. (Nietzsche 1911: 151).

Thus the politics of transfiguration implies transfiguration of values. What transfigures values if not forces? Forces are the fictional, figurative—in other words, aesthetic—essence of the will to power that selects, shapes, forms and creates new possibilities of life by overcoming given values which have become decadent, and transforms given values into something life-affirming and life-enhancing. It is in this sense we say that force is what is to be introduced—and this is what remained unthought in metaphysics of grammar—into the political: to introduce force—its rhythm and melody—is to introduce the value and sense of transfiguration, to create and form out of the formless, to give 'a unity of artistic styles'. In other words, to create the condition of culture is to give music to the people: this is the foremost political task for us who are abandoned by the God of onto-theological grammar.

NOTES

1. I refer to Martin Heidegger's discussion of it in 'A Dialogue on Language' (Heidegger 1971: 6).
2. Thus we allude to Plato's determination of Being as *Morphē* which comes from the metaphysical distinction between what and that (*essentia* and *existentia*). The present day linguist's distinction between surface and deep structure already presupposes this metaphysical distinction.
3. Martin Heidegger remarks: 'Of late, the scientific and philosophical investigation of languages is aiming ever more resolutely at the production of what is called "metalanguage". Analytical philosophy, which is set on producing this super-language, is quite consistent when it considers itself metalinguistics. That sounds like metaphysics—not only sounds like this, it is metaphysics. Metalinguistics is the metaphysics of the thoroughgoing technicalization of all languages into the sole operative instrument of interplanetary information.

Metalanguage and sputnik, metalinguistics and rocketry are the same' (Heidegger 1971: 58).

4. It would be necessary for us to undertake a deconstructive reading of the entire metaphysical determination of time as presence to show that the metaphysical determination of the temporal closure amount to the repression of the melodic and rhythmic forces of language for the sake of concept and that this repression is the condition of the possibility of the "political" based on the basis of the grammatical-dialectical modality of thought. Thus, to allude here to Husserl's phenomenological determination of the internal time-consciousness on the basis of musical experience, Husserl's temporal closure in the name of retention and protention as the attenuated variation of presence, represses or does not account for resonance which is (im)properly musical that itself cannot be accounted in the name of retention and protention (Husserl 1981: 277-93). The same thing occurs in Freud's inability to account musical experience—its rhythm and melodic forces—with the help of his libidinal theory (Freud did not like music. Would it amount to a repression itself: another repression, more primordial than repression of our sexual drives based on Oedipus Complex?). For a discussion of Freud's confrontation with Reik about the problem of musical experience, see Philippe Lacoue-Labarthe's 'The Echo of the Subject' (Lacoue-Labarthe 1998). Here Lacoue-Labarthe shows that this repression of musicality is nothing but the problem of the "Subject": the whole metaphysical determination of the political is at stake here.

REFERENCES

Heidegger, Martin, *On the Way to Language*, trans. Peter D. Hertz (New York, Evanston: Harper and Row, 1971).

Husserl, Edmund, "The Phenomenology of Internal Time Consciousness" in *Husserl: Shorter Works*, ed. Peter McCormick and Frederick A. Elliston (Indiana: University of Notre Dame Press and The Harvester Press, 1981).

Lacoue-Labarthe, Philippe, "The Echo of the Subject" in *Typography: Mimesis, Philosophy, Politics*, ed. Christopher Fynsk (Stanford and California: Stanford University Press, 1998).

Nietzsche, Friedrich, "On the Uses and Disadvantages of History for Life" in *Untimely Meditations*, trans. R.J. Hollingdale (Cambridge: Cambridge University Press, 1997).

Nietzsche, Friedrich, "On Music and Words", an appendix to Carl Dahlhaus' *Between Romanticism and Modernism: Four Studies in the Music in the Later 19th Century*, trans. Mary Whittall (Berkeley: University of California Press, 1980).

Nietzsche, Friedrich, *Selected Letters of Friedrich Nietzsche*, ed. and trans. Christopher Middleton (Chicago and London: Chicago University Press, 1969).

Nietzsche, Friedrich, *Twilight of the Idols* and *The Anti-Christ*, trans. R.J. Hollingdale (Harmondsworth: Penguin Books, 1968).

Nietzsche, Friedrich, *The Birth of Tragedy and The Case of Wagner*, trans. Walter Kaufmann (New York: Vintage Books, 1967).

Nietzsche, Friedrich, *The Dawn of Day*, tr. J.M Kennedy (London: George Allen & Unwin Ltd, 1911).